FRANK RYAN, Ph.D.

SPORTS AND PSYCHOLOGY

PRENTICE-HALL, INC., Englewood Cliffs, New Jersey

For Vivian M. Ryan

Sports and Psychology by Frank Ryan, Ph.D.
Copyright © 1981 by Frank Ryan
All right reserved. No part of this book may be
reproduced in any form or by any means, except
for the inclusion of brief quotations in a review,
without permission in writing from the publisher.
Address inquiries to Prentice-Hall, Inc., Englewood Cliffs, N.J. 07632
Printed in the United States of America
Prentice-Hall International, Inc., London
Prentice-Hall of Australia, Pty. Ltd., Sydney
Prentice-Hall of Canada, Ltd., Toronto
Prentice-Hall of India Private Ltd., New Delhi
Prentice-Hall of Japan, Inc., Tokyo
Prentice-Hall of Southeast Asia Pt. Ltd., Singapore
Whitehall Books Limited, Wellington, New Zealand

10   9   8   7   6   5   4   3   2   1

Library of Congress Cataloging in Publication Data

Ryan, Frank.
Sports and psychology.

Includes index.
1.   Sports—Psychological aspects.   I.   Title.
GV706.4.R9   796'.01   81–5108
ISBN 0-13-837856-8   AACR2
ISBN 0-13-837849-5 (pbk)

Introduction

The movement called sports psychology is new and blossoming. It is gathering momentum, as indicated by the many societies, meetings, and publications that are springing up all over the world. For each person who expressed an interest in the psychology of sports a generation ago there are probably a thousand today. The movement is so rapid and has become so large that it's difficult to either explain its roots or to characterize it.

We might try the thesis that two significant areas of human behavior are reaching toward each other to form a new science. Sports activity is old and fundamental, and so is interest in human behavior. Perhaps a joining of the two was one day inevitable. Maybe so. But such a thesis somehow seems naive.

Let's consider some of the movement's possible roots. It was about twenty years ago that I first heard some sort of psychological phrases from prominent athletes. The most frequently used expressions were "psych up," which was what they meant to do to themselves, and "psych out," which was what they wanted to do to their opponents. I don't think it was entirely a use of psychological jargon. Though most of the athletes probably had little acquaintance with the formal science of psychology, what they had in mind when they used these phases possessed a strong note of reality. They knew that there were ways to get themselves prepared for more effective performances, and they knew there were ways to decrease the effectiveness of their opponents.

As for the coaches, it's hard to know what part they played in the new movement. I knew many of them, and it's my impression that the early coaches were unusually shrewd in their perceptions of human behavior, and exercised a rough and ready "practical psychology." Because the early coaches had little formal education, they had very little contact with college faculties. They may have had no contact with the psychologists. Even if they had, it probably would not have done much good. The old coaches had a distrust of academicians, and the psychologists had very little interest in or knowledge of athletics. The coaches of today have university degrees and can therefore enter the academic picture much more readily than could their predecessors. Still, I don't think the modern coach is much more psychologically oriented than the nonacademic coaches of the past. His basic attitude is "Give me the horses"—that is, give me every aid in recruiting talented athletes. Yet he knows that there is something in the air and feels that he cannot take the chance of being left out of the sports psychology movement. He cannot afford to miss a possible "edge."

Though the majority of athletic coaches seem to have a "wait and see" attitude toward the new emphasis on the use of psychology in sports, a few have a more optimistic and pioneering view. Some of this minority have even expressed the opinion that we have reached the point of diminishing returns in the development of athletic techniques. They believe that nearly all coaches are or shortly will be about equal in mastery of techniques. Therefore, they believe, both advances in performances and advantages in competition will have to come about along psychological lines. Such a millennium has not really arrived, but the idea of applying psychology more often seems good. The great driving force behind the sports psychology movement seems to be exerted by the physical educators. They are the ones who organize meetings, arrange for publications, and teach the courses in sports psychology. If the physical educators comprise the main force, as seems to be the case, several considerations arise. The orientation of the physical educator is, I feel, different from that of the coach. Though the two disciplines overlap—some physical educators coach and some coaches teach physical education—there is a chasm between them. The physical educator emphasizes sports participation and the benefits derived from it. He tends to speak in terms of health, expression of the body, and personality growth. The coach, on the other hand, is directed toward winning and achieving. In short, the real difference between them is the premium they place on victory in competition. There is a bias on both sides. However, when their differences are aired, it is the physical educator who is more likely to be heard. Unlike the coach, the physical educator is familiar with the academic system of courses, credits, and faculty publications. Physical educators could be misleading in setting up courses that are not realistic. We already have the doubtful situation in which people who have neither coached nor become acquainted with psychology are teaching sports psychology and contributing to the journals.

What of the psychologists? I suppose it would take a survey to find out how much impetus is being given to sports psychology by the psychologists themselves. My impression is that it's very little. The traditional academic psychologist has not been oriented toward sports. For the most part he does not know one sport from another and would have trouble finding his way to the stadium or the practice fields. That, however, can change. With a proper and pleasant introduction to sports he may, like the rest of us, succumb to their sheer delight and become a fan. He could develop an interest in sports without ever including them in his professional activities. But who knows? Sports offer such a rich and dramatic source of data about human behavior that it might compel research interest. If I were to guess, I would say that early contributions to sports psychology will come from applied psychology and perhaps clinical psychology. Later on, more Copernican insights will come from the theorists.

The word "psychology" is surely one of the most baffling and fascinating terms in the language. It is used by just about everyone. The universal usage of this word reflects man's need to know something about man and his behavior. The word "psychology" touches off different "feels" in different people. To the professional psychologist it may mean a rather specific area and a certain scientific methodology. But even among the professionals there are widely varying notions about what psychology is. Many theorists are horrified that the clinical psychologists think of psychology as a treatment process. As for the person whom we condescendingly call the "layman," he really doesn't use the term "psychology" in an entirely random and nebulous manner. For him, not every mental event is psychological. He would not, for example, consider a mathematician puzzling over a problem as being involved in a psychological process. The layman's concepts of psychology apparently lie in rough-and-ready predicting and influencing of behavior. In this respect he is really not too far apart from many professional psychologists. The great differences separating the layman and the professional result from formal training. Foremost, I think, is the professional's feeling that psychology must be a science. He knows its history. He clings to methodology. He knows that psychology cannot make the long and defeatist retreat to speculative philosophy. It's no longer enough to sit around the cracker barrel and listen to the observations of shrewd observers. For the professional there has to be a substance to psychology in the forms of method and some sort of hard-won body of knowledge.

Psychology means many things to many people. What I have been suggesting, of course, is that the orientation and the direction of the rapidly expanding sports psychology movement will depend upon the people who become dominant in the field—those who teach the courses, write the journal articles and books, and plan the meetings. At present, it seems that these people will operate in isolation from formal psychology. If this happens, sports psychology would amount to a literary collection of shrewd observations and anecdotes about successful coaches and athletes. That's not all bad. Any procedure that draws attention to the human relations aspect of sports participation has to have some virtue. However, a dead end is indicated. Operating apart from formal psychology, the sports psychologists would find themselves in the anachronistic position of Socrates in the marketplace. Socrates did astonishingly well, but two thousand years should bring us new and improved approaches.

Will there be a strong interaction between sports psychology and formal psychology? I think so, but not right away. It's rare for a coach or physical educator to have an extensive background in psychology, and it's even more unusual for a psychologist to have a background in sports. Hence, it will probably be a long time before there is a vigorous and meaningful interaction between sports and formal psychology. For a time to come both the person in sports and the psychologist will tend to view each other as "men from Mars."

There are many psychologies. The psychologies that I talk about in this book are the ones I think have the most significance for sports psychology. In this selection process my prejudices show. I regard the dynamic psychologies as representing an enormous breakthrough in our views of human nature. Thus, attention has to be given to the revelations of Freud, and to those who followed him and opposed him. Next, since coaches, athletes, and physical educators are always closely involved with the learning process, it's appropriate to take a look at some of the concepts that have been developed in the area of learning. Experimental work with animals has supplied the bases for most of the significant learning theories. So we have to see what the animals have been doing. Third, sports psychology has already become deeply involved in personality theory and personality testing procedures. This involvement is surely going to increase. Hence, we ought to know something about the nature of personality tests.

You will notice that I have not put the science of psychology on a pedestal. Though a hard look is needed, it is not my intention to minimize the struggles and the brilliant efforts made by so many intelligent and dedicated people. Rather, the intention is to underscore the difficulties inherent in a scientific effort to study human nature. As more and more people in sports turn toward psychology, their assessments of psychology and what it can offer ought to be realistic. Magical expectations usually lead to disenchantment.

This is not a "how-to" book for either coaches or athletes. For the most part I've avoided prescriptions. In the few instances where I have given in to the temptation to offer advice, there were, I think, special grounds. Whenever a procedure is compellingly suggested by the congruence of theoretical views and my more than twenty years of face-to-face coaching, it seems reasonable to pass that procedure along for consideration.

I would like to make several of the prejudices I mentioned above explicit. First, I don't think there can be much of a sports psychology at all unless there is a hookup with formal psychology. Those who will teach sports psychology have a special obligation to become well acquainted with the science of psychology. Second, sports psychology ought to have the same goals as other sciences. There ought to be a pure and systematic search for knowledge. On the applied side, the goal should be to contribute to a richer experience for those involved in sports. Exploitation of any athlete should be definitely out of bounds. Third, sports ought to be fun. If pushed for an explanation of what I mean by that, I'd have trouble answering, just as I would be at a loss if some humorless person asked me to explain why a particular joke is funny. I suppose I mean that sports should remain unique and continue to offer us a special kind of delight. Because of this prejudice I find it impossible to fall in step with those who would attack the problems of sports psychology in grim and dreary fashion. The grim ones will, I think, regard me as somewhat frivolous at times.

Contents

Introduction *iii*

About Sports *1*

About Psychology *12*

Little Church Around the Couch *23*

Ask the Animals *44*

Figuring Out Personality *63*

The Coach *82*

The Coach and the Athlete *96*

Who Will Do Well? *113*

A Pattern Named Desire *129*

Regression Under Stress *142*

Retroactive Inhibition *147*

Role Playing *152*

Mental Rehearsal *159*

Errors of Anticipation *165*

Psychological Limits *176*

Observation *186*

Those Who Cannot Compete *192*

An Added Word *221*

Index *223*

About Sports

It would be highly desirable if we could start with a precise definition of sports and sports behavior. But I doubt that we can come up with a definition that would be truly useful. In general, definitions dealing with human behavior have become more difficult. We would have been more comfortable with definitions when we were more naive and the world seemed less complex. If we were living in medieval Europe, for example, a definition of religious activity would have been nearly complete had it included carrying out God's will, getting to heaven, and avoiding hell. Today, most men of the cloth would feel useless and idle if these were their main goals. We might even have defined sexual behavior in the pre-Freudian era.

Though useful definitions of sports behavior in the classical sense seem likely to elude us, the area does have special characteristics that we can pinpoint. It is true that if we examine any single characteristic we tend to find that this particular characteristic is shared by other areas of behavior. Yet it seems likely that no other human activity

1

shares *all* that characterizes sports behavior. Hence, the sum of its characteristics can for our purposes set sports behavior apart.

Universality / Sports seem to thrive best in an affluent and "civilized" society. The ancient Greeks are pointed to as the first society to glorify sports striving, and the legacy of legend and tradition are still important to us. Today, the United States and Russia are the athletic powerhouses.

There is a correlation between national wealth and sports activity. Explanations of this correlation have been advanced. The most familiar one is that when at least a good part of the population can get rid of the need to scrounge for a living, many of them will turn to the arts if given the opportunity—and sports is an art form. This view is, I believe, valid in a certain sense. Wealth and leisure may not initiate athletic behavior, but they surely can help to sustain it. Anywhere on earth, if given even a slight chance, youngsters will play. There will be games regardless of the economic situation. But the child may have the grim task of helping with the family's struggle for a living, and be unable to give the time and effort that sports proficiency requires.

If a nation is to perform well on the international sports scene there has to be a method of singling out the promising youngsters and giving them the benefits of money and leisure. All that means, of course, is taking everyday financial burdens off their backs so that they have a chance of reaching their athletic potential. The usual methods of most nations to allow an athlete a full opportunity to train are outright subsidies and soft government jobs. In this way, regardless of his former economic position, he gains some of the advantages of the aristocrat of olden times. The United States, the richest nation of all

time, has a subsidy method that bewilders sports authorities in other parts of the world. American sports are
uniquely built around the academic institutions. The fed-
eral government has no direct participation in athletic
subsidies—not yet, anyway.

The pull of sports is so powerful that even under-
developed nations are coming up with great athletes. In
Africa particularly we have seen the emergence of Olympic
champions and world record holders who have astonished
us all. We know now that even a poor nation can, if it
wishes, supply a few outstanding athletes with the needed
leisure and facilities to train, and in this way simulate the
situation of the aristocrat of yore.

Our main point is that sports activity is universal. The
tendency to play does seem innate and it may be sustained
or it may be chopped off. The sustenance, whatever its
source, is eventually reduced by maturation or the aging
process. But nevertheless, the tendency to play or to perform in sports is there in the first place. It is a legacy. The
term "human nature" has had its ups and downs. At the
moment, it seems to be on the downswing. If you mention
the term to a fairly serious university student, his training
forces him to regard you as a primitive. Because of our
academic approach the term "human nature" is anathema
to most students. They have been taught to believe that
environment accounts for nearly all of human behavior,
that innate patterns do not exist. Though the environmentalists are leery of conceding the existence of such a
business as "human nature," what do they think about
infrahumans? Is there a "bird nature" or a "spider
nature"? Birds appear able to build nests without environ-
mental influence. Spiders spin their webs without
instruction.

The environmentalists have enjoyed a long day and are

ascendent, but they do say that some behavior may be an expression of human nature. But if any pattern of human behavior is to be considered human nature, three criteria have to be strictly observed: (1) universality, (2) biological continuity, and (3) physiological base. These are tough criteria, but they can be satisfied as far as sports behavior is concerned. Universality, of course, means that the behavior should pop up regardless of culture. Biological continuity means that the activity under consideration can be observed among the infrahumans. The third criterion suggests that the behavior under consideration has to derive from some bodily mechanism. All in all, these three criteria comprise a stern test of what really is human nature. They are too tough, I think, for most of human behavior, but as far as sports activity is concerned, the criteria can be met. Take a look at each of the criteria as they apply to sports.

To me, universality would stand by itself. We would not need the others. As far as I know, there is no culture in which the young do not engage in play activity. As for the other two criteria, though not needed, they seem to be satisfied. We know that animals, at least when young, do show play activity. The physiological base for play activity is probably related to the growth process.

For the young / Participation in sports is for the young and relatively young. Especially is this true of the vigorous sports such as track, football, soccer, wrestling, and hockey. The harsh fact is that we peak physically at a certain age, and after that it's all downhill. The course of the parabola is inexorable. The slope of the downhill part can be made less steep, but the general pattern cannot be stopped.

Nearly all athletes give up serious competition before they reach their physical peaks. The relatively few who continue on to and past their peaks almost always have extraordinary talent and other incentives such as money and fame. They tend to extend their careers past their physical peak in a number of ways. First, they may be so very good that even when their physical abilities begin to fade, they are still good enough to perform comparatively well. Second, they can flatten the slope of decline through special physical efforts. Third, they can partially compensate for loss of speed and strength by increased skill. But there are limits to what can be done. The aging process inevitably has its result.

The sports in which a person can function well beyond his physical peak are those in which the contestant supplies no *direct* energy. The swimmer or the runner, for example, must supply all of the propulsion. In contrast, the members of a yachting crew, though they may work very hard, supply no direct propulsion to the yacht. The oldest member of an Olympic team seems always to be a yachtsman.

Sports like track and field and swimming require both youth and top physical condition. It isn't enough to be "young at heart." So, the basic sports involve: how fast? how high? how far? In a sense they amount to tests of what the body can do. It seems a little pathetic to test the body in these ways after its physical peak has been passed.

The process of aging as it relates to sports participation deserves treatment far beyond the scope of this book. The topic of "lifetime sports" is beginning to get the attention that it should have. Surely, people should continue to participate in sports as long as they wish. It's just that there comes a time in life when a new psychological approach to sports is indicated.

No product / The butcher, the baker, and the candlestick maker all create products. And so do people in most occupations. But in sports no product emerges, and none is contemplated. This feature of sports distinguishes it from most other things we do in life, an interesting fact in view of the vast energy given over to sports. Lack of product distinguishes sports not only from the everyday world of work but from most of the other arts as well. There is no painting, no musical composition, no sculpture, no poem. The psychological implications of there being no product in sports might be highly complicated, but, as a starter, there is the suggestion that sport begins as a play activity with no other goal in mind.

Artificial difficulties / In sports we do more than tolerate obstacles. We purposely set them up to see how well we can overcome them. The hurdles race is a prime example. The task is to get from the starting line to the finish line as fast as possible, but a series of hurdles is placed between these two points. Without these obstacles there would, of course, be no event. In golf the notion of using clubs to get a ball in a hole that is several hundred yards away is in itself contrived. But additional obstacles have been devised such as doglegs, sand traps, roughs, and water hazards. An industrialist would not place obstacles in his factory just to see how well he can handle them. A farmer would not place rocks in his fields to see how well he can plow around them. The artificial obstacles seem unique to sports. They apparently reflect both play and personal testing.

Amateur and professional / A recent and highly striking development has been the emergence of the highly paid professional athlete. It wasn't long ago that professional football players played to almost empty stadiums and for their efforts in a game received checks for a hundred dollars or less—checks, incidentally, that would often bounce. Today, yearly incomes of six figures are common in many sports, including football, basketball, baseball, and hockey. Top golfers and tennis players earn half a million dollars a year and up. More than a few professional athletes are millionaires. Boxing was the precursor of the money flow. Even generations ago fortunes were made in boxing, but only by the top heavyweights. Among the smaller men, the ex-greats often support themselves with menial jobs.

In any consideration of sports behavior it would be foolish to ignore the colossi of professional sports that have sprung up among us. The professional sports are now the most popular, whether football in the United States or soccer elsewhere. The spectacular rise of professionalism has to have some impact on our notions of sports psychology, but we have to be careful not to overestimate its effects. In the very early stages of sports participation, really play, the enormous prestige of professional sports probably has very little direct effect. The tots will throw a ball, run, and play tag and other games. They won't have thoughts of becoming great professional athletes. Even if there were no television or professional sports they would play at games. It's only when the child grows older that professional sports begin to influence behavior.

Put briefly, the exciting and dramatic professional sports contests, even though they rivet the attention of the adult world, probably have no influence on the child's early play or sports behavior. Play efforts in childhood appear to result from a biological and psychological legacy. When a child first turns to sports it seems most unlikely that he has any plans for making money from them. Later on, however, as the child matures and experiences more of life, his motivation to participate in sports becomes multi-determined. It is then that the youngsters are influenced by the heroes that professional sports provide. Fantasies of gold, prestige, and a new way of life begin to entice them.

The carrot is before the nose. Though great professional athletes have risen from the ghetto to become wealthy, the odds of that happening are bad. For more than 99 percent, imitation of the great and wealthy professionals has to remain a fantasy.

It seems to me that the main effect of the great rise of professionalism is to keep the athlete going longer than he otherwise would have. Professionals in all sports would have played early in their lives even if there had been no possibility of making money from these activities. They started by playing simply for the fun of it. All that money has done is to sustain the activity. The average old football pro will have aches and pains and a decreased desire to undergo the day's training program. Nevertheless, he will still get up and do the job for which he has contracted. He probably continues to get satisfaction from his sport but has the suspicion that his sports activity might best be carried out on a different basis. He senses that it would be more appropriate for him to switch to the lifetime sports. At a certain physiological and psychological age, high-powered athletic participation ought to give way to perhaps a round of golf or a few sets of doubles in tennis. It should be pointed out, however, that the violent competitor should probably not engage in any sport after age forces him to retire from his area of greatness—unless he can make a rather radical psychological adjustment. If he brings his old ferocious will to win to lifetime sports, he is likely to suffer. There would be no relaxation. More important, he would probably do himself serious physical harm.

Perhaps a good deal more will be discovered about the impact of professionalism on sports behavior. For the moment, however, it seems that two of its aspects are significant. First, because of the enormous publicity that the professional superstars get, they tend to be heroes to the youngsters. The greats supply a source of motivation for the young athletes after the original biological base is on the wane and mixed with other motives. Second, to the delight of the fans, professionalism lengthens the careers of the beloved top and colorful athletes. Both of these effects produced by the spectacular rise of professional sports would appear to be benign.

There are still some crusaders for the "amateur ideal" who are nourished by their own feelings of virtue and the tributes of their followers. But today, the tributes lessen, and the crusader is increasingly regarded as quaint, or as an outright nuisance and bore. Often the publicized crusader for amateurism is a man of wealth, and the actual policing of amateurism is carried out by hired hands who occupy the curious position of getting paid by sports interests to prevent other people from making money from sports. The old amateur values are still officially accepted under international rules. Most nations, however, have smoothly circumvented the anachronistic code with very little open confrontation. The United States officials have probably been the most naive of all in carrying out the unrealistic task of policing amateurism. Can anyone really believe that we can impose the traditions of a nineteenth-century English country gentleman upon the apprentice working in a Russian factory or the youngster living in an American ghetto!

Masculine striving / Sports that require youth, fitness, and strength have generally been regarded as forms of masculine striving. Some psychiatrists who have athletes as patients are convinced that masculine striving is central to athletic motivation. Moreover, they feel that the real motivation comes from the fear of not being masculine enough. There may be some validity to this view in some cases. But the clinical samples may not be representative, and they are likely to be small, since athletes are not inclined to seek psychiatric help. It is possible that even the most masculine and rugged-appearing athlete may have some doubts, conscious or unconscious, about his masculinity. However, other athletes may not have such doubts. But either way, there is the suggestion that masculine striving is an aspect of athletics that should be taken into account in the psychological exploration of sports behavior. It would, however, be misleading to assume that all sports involve masculine striving to the same extent. Each sport has to be treated separately.

If we are to assume that masculine striving is an essential characteristic of at least some sports, what do we make of the recent great influx of females into sports? Large numbers of females are entering nearly all sports, including those traditionally considered strictly male territories. Still, we have to know more about what is really going on. This striking movement of females into sports deserves intensive research efforts. And these efforts would seem bound to be highly complex.

The mass movement of females into some sports may represent a symbolic protest more than a realistic effort to compete on equal terms with males. In the entire history of the Olympic Games no female would even have qualified to compete if there had not been separate divisions for men and women. In the shot put, for example, the men's shot is twice as heavy as the eight-pounder used by women. Yet the men still put much farther than women. Our very top female track and field athletes would not have the slightest chance of placing in a championship meet for schoolboys.

Attempts at a definition / It has been traditional for scholars to attempt definitions of an area prior to examining it. In the sports area, however, an academic definition would not seem to be useful and might even be misleading. To be sufficiently inclusive it would have to be extended to the point of being unwieldy. I think, at present, our best bet is simply to try to take account of some of the distinctive features of sports in formulating our analyses and research approaches.

About Psychology

Though disciplines such as economics, history, or physiology are of necessity concerned with human behavior, psychology alone has the unique and difficult task of directly and comprehensively examining behavior. The scientific study of mankind may be about as difficult a task as mankind can find. Has any other scientific effort produced so much frustration?

The amateurs / There are very few amateur physicists or amateur chemists, but there are about as many amateur psychologists as there are people. Mankind's ability to function and even to survive depends upon a certain amount of accuracy in understanding and predicting human behavior. It was surely so for the caveman, and it is so for us in today's complex societies.

For most people survival is literally tied up with occupation. Our ability to feed, clothe, and house ourselves is related to our performance on the job. There are, of course, some jobs that require very little understanding of human behavior. For example, the artisan who works alone may function with relatively little knowledge of human behavior. But most jobs do require an ability to assess and predict human behavior. The successful used car salesman has gotten good at sizing up potential customers. The con man at the carnival appears able to read the people he can take advantage of. At present, it would be very difficult to offer advice to these people on the basis of experimental findings in psychology. So it is with the successful athletic coach. He deals with athletes day in and day out and is certainly not completely naive about their behavior. In fact, many coaches are rather shrewd about assessing personality—at least, within the framework in which they operate. The contributions of formal psychology to the coach, in order to be useful to him, have to be above and beyond what he is able to perceive on his own.

It would seem to be difficult to evaluate the "psychological knowledge" of the apparently well-functioning amateur. If he indeed does function well, one has to assume a certain amount of validity. However, the "psychology" used by the amateur seems to be made up of all manner of things ranging from intuitive feelings to a welter of axioms or slogans. The repertory of axioms is bound to contain some nonsense and contradictions.

The early professionals / Even before the ancient Greeks, primitive societies probably had specialists who were consulted for advice on both personal and general matters. We do know that the Greek philosophers, including Plato and Aristotle, formulated theories of human nature. The methodology of the Greek philosophers consisted mainly of a cycle of observation–speculation–dialogue–observation.

Philosophers continued to be the formal spokesmen for psychology for many centuries to come. That was natural enough, since they assumed a proprietorship of all sciences.

Astronomy, physics, and chemistry all left the parental fold of philosophy during the sixteenth and seventeenth centuries. Biology stayed another century before it too went on its own. Psychology remained a part of philosophy until near the end of the nineteenth century, but long before it broke away there were efforts to apply the emerging views of chemistry and physics to human behavior (e.g., the work of Descartes). Psychology's delay in leaving philosophy was no doubt due to a number of factors. One reason, I suspect, may have been the similarity in temperament and outlook between philosophers and psychologists. For example, even the great thinker William James, who wrote *Principles of Psychology*, started as a philosopher, became a psychologist, and then returned to philosophy. The most frequently cited reason for psychology's break with philosophy is the growth and influence of physiology. Physiology's methods seemed appropriate to an experimental psychology, and so was its subject matter. The first experimental psychologists operated within a framework of stimulus and mental process (in modern times it became stimulus and response). Great emphasis was placed upon the receptors. That still seems a logical move. If we are to understand an organism's behavior we have to know something about the input from its environment.

By about 1890 psychologists were able to get professorships, and departments were being established in the universities. After these beachheads were won, the advance of psychology as an independent science was rapid.

As of today / The great early growth of psychology was within university settings with departments and larger staffs springing up everywhere. In the early part of this century, psychologists accepted, at least formally, a definition that limited their study to the consciousness. Interest shifted from the examination of conscious experiences to actual behavior. This shift flared into open revolt, and "schools" began to emerge and consolidate themselves. The better known schools produced by the revolution are behaviorism, Gestalt psychology, and psychoanalysis. Psychoanalysis was different from the other schools in that it arose outside of the academic framework. It was a medical treatment. Yet its impact on academia was enormous. Psychologists were not the only ones who felt there was something wrong with our faith in the consciousness of the "rational man" as the sole determinant of man's action. So did economists, historians, philosophers, poets, and sociologists. All had long sensed, at least vaguely, that we had been lacking an essential factor in our efforts to understand mankind. Obviously, the emergence of a brilliant and highly articulated system such as psychoanalysis had to have its welcome. But other schools of psychology more than survive. In general, it can be said that the schools represent different orientations in terms of theories, approaches, and methodologies. The complexity of human behavior apparently demands this diversity.

The enormous increase in the numbers of professional psychologists was related to two significant patterns. At one time, psychologists could support themselves only as teachers in the universities. But other areas of human striving began to look to psychology for an "edge." It was felt that the human factors may have a decisive effect on all manner of enterprises—as, of course, they do. The feeling, often mixed, was that if we can hire psychologists, they will bring us an advantage. As a result, psychologists began to spill into nearly every major area of human activity, including education, the military, law, industry, psychotherapy, and advertising. The other pattern was the emergence of specialties. Among the well-worked fields of psychology are physiological, child, comparative, personality, social, genetic, applied, educational, and abnormal. As suggested, psychology is no longer a simple discipline in which a few scholars engage in efforts to find out how the "mind works." To know only that a person is a psychologist gives you practically no information about his interests or day-to-day professional activities.

The "catch-up" game / Human behavior has gotten the attention of just about every person who has ever lived. Even the mentally defective and the psychotic are sometimes good at sizing up some aspects of personality. They often show uncanny sensitivity toward another person's attitudes. In nearly all groups views of human nature are expressed in folklore. Among the billions who have tried to puzzle out human nature, only a few great minds have become immortal. Their views, expressed in plays, novels, poems, and essays, are still with us. For example, the profound insights of Shakespeare are quoted today by psychologists and psychiatrists.

It would seem that psychology is much more an approach or method than it is a body of knowledge. In its origin as a separate discipline psychology represented an act of faith in science. It was a revolt from the notion that wise and learned men alone could advance our understanding of human nature by speculation. It was believed that a new approach had to be tried if psychology were truly to become a science. And that new approach was experimentation. Early experimental methods were concerned with sensation and perception, certainly a logical start by almost any definition of psychology. Also, "higher" processes such as memory and learning appeared amenable to the experimental method. The results of these early efforts were encouraging enough to reinforce the optimistic belief that in time all problems in psychology could be approached successfully via the experimental method.

Those psychologists who have not been distracted or who have not otherwise given up are still optimistic about their chances of formulating a scientific understanding of human behavior. They are inclined to concede that in many areas of behavior there is an obvious scientific lag, but they do feel that scientific psychology will eventually catch up to and surpass the common-sense psychology that has been amassed over countless generations.

Some realities / The professional education of the aspiring psychologist would appear to be somewhat different from that of graduate students in other sciences. A graduate student in biology, physics, chemistry, or astronomy participates more in a body of knowledge including facts and theories. In these sciences many of the correlations afford surefire predictability. The student learns things that are far beyond the ken of even the brightest of laymen, and he can thus perform in ways that the layman cannot. Of course, this situation also holds true for the professional schools, such as medicine, law, or engineering.

The education or training of the graduate student in psychology seems to depend very heavily and almost capriciously upon the institution he attends. The courses that he takes and the research that he undertakes will depend upon the special qualifications and interests of the faculty members.

The motivations to become a psychologist must surely vary widely from student to student. There are those who enter graduate school because of inferiority feelings, either mental or physical or both. If the feeling of inferiority is mental there is the illusion that a graduate degree can help by certifying intelligence. If there is a feeling of physical inferiority, the motivation may be to get a leveller, or "edge." Of course, there is also the practical motive of acquiring the formal qualifications for finding a snug and secure spot at a college, a school system, or elsewhere. Investigation would likely reveal a wide range of motives, many of which would not appear "pure" or "noble." But that's no reason to decry them. After all, the sadist may become a respected surgeon and the masochist a revered saint.

The most puzzled graduate student of all in the psychology department will be the one who genuinely—and naively—expects to learn something about human nature. But this type can usually be kept busy and worried enough to distract him from his original notion of learning about human nature. One hurdle after another is placed in his path. The language requirements for a Ph.D. degree amount to pure hurdles. The student must pass two foreign-language examinations, though it is tacitly assumed that he will never really use these languages in his scientific reading. The nature of other hurdles will depend largely upon the interests of the faculty members. Training is likely to include statistics, tests and measurements, experimental design, the mathematics of rational equations, physiology, comparative psychology. The emphasis given each subject will reflect the special interest and abilities of individual members of the faculty. For example, at one great university a faculty member was a world-famous expert on vision. Every candidate for the doctorate was required to take a most intensive course in vision. This requirement was surely a happenstance and not the result of a rational master plan of what the graduate student should study. There is no denying the expertise of many specialists who are in a formal sense psychologists. But this expertise often lies in an area that at best would seem only peripheral to psychology. It does not seem unfair to raise the question of whether these scientists are really psychologists even if they are members of a psychology department. Could it be that great expertise in a specialty that is only remotely connected with human nature is the reaction of a brilliant mentality to frustration? Is there a feeling that human nature cannot really be understood via the methods used in the physical sciences?

At some institutions the training of a psychologist is more practical and less academic or scientific. Here the budding psychologist is being groomed to carry out the functions of a working professional. The emphasis may be on psychotherapy and counseling. Or if the stress is on tests and measurements the student is probably being readied for a career in applied psychology—clinical, industrial, educational, or other. The training, strongly influenced by the orientation of the teachers, is designed to impart what is considered a body of knowledge and methods. Once learned, this "body" is used on the job. However, such training is not calculated to produce students who purely pursue an understanding of human nature. Curiosity, original thinking, and bold research are rare.

Product and influence / We are surrounded and influenced by the tangible products that have sprung from the physical sciences—aircraft, television, automobiles. We also have the myriad products engendered by the atomic age and space exploration—and, of course, we have the computer. The countless products of the physical sciences have radically changed our everyday lives. Philosophical ideas have also had great impact on us, especially when they became translated into religious and political movements—e.g., Christianity and communism. But in the case of scientific psychology influence on everyday life is hard to find. No products have been developed that are in use by the general public. At least for the present, it appears that our lives would be pretty much the same if scientific psychology had not evolved. Still, it may be early in the game.

Most sciences have produced or have been fortunate enough to have had one or more geniuses who have had tremendous impact not only on their own scientific community but on other disciplines and, eventually, on society at large. Copernicus, Galileo, Faraday, Einstein, and Darwin quickly come to mind. If psychology has had a figure of comparable stature and influence it would have to have been the great genius, Sigmund Freud. But the results are not all in yet. Freud's views surely have many critics, some of them violent in their opposition. Even some of his disciples were in strong disagreement with him. Nevertheless, Freudian views have strongly affected the practice of psychiatry and, perhaps to a lesser extent, the thinking of psychologists. It does seem that literature and jurisprudence too have been influenced by the thought of the famous Viennese neurologist. However, it is difficult to know the extent to which Freudian views have affected the average man.

Stimulus and response / The early scientific psychologists were greatly concerned with stimulus and the correlated sensation and perception. Their approach was heavily influenced by physiology, from which they borrowed. In fact, some of the early psychologists were also physiologists. It was their preoccupation with "internal experience" that brought about one of the major revolts. The behaviorists felt that in order to progress from a philosophical exercise to a science, psychology had to ignore the events taking place within the organism. The correlations between stimulus and response were considered the only proper data.

It is difficult for the layman to understand how a science of human behavior can be advanced by methodologically ignoring a vital source of data. It seems limiting, if not defeating, to look at the functioning of anything in that way, from a motor car to a television set to a computer. Knowing something about the relationship between input and output is useful, but someone has to know about the "insides." A psychology that concentrates strictly on stimulus and response, which originally aroused excitement and optimism, does seem to have had its high noon. Future progress in our understanding of human nature may depend on discoveries made in the mathematico–biophysical field.

Divisions / The American Psychological Association is characterized by its many formal divisions. It was inevitable that psychologists would cluster in accordance with their interests, training, and activities. Those in the same special field have much in common and feel their collegial communication is enhanced by being in the same compartment. However, it does seem that rigid compartmentalization can present some potential difficulties. Burying oneself in a specialty may in many instances represent an escape from any obligation to make a contribution to our understanding of human nature. Contentment and absorption with the everyday activities within the specialty may obscure any overall goal. Much of the research within a compartment is either empirical or concerned with minor hypotheses. It seldom relates to comprehensive theories of human nature. Worse yet, those who simply administer tests and score them in accordance with the instructions in a manual are reduced to being technicians.

If there is to be a progressive and vital sports psychology, interested people in sports will have to turn to formal psychology to find it. At present, however, the turning will have to be in the direction of one or more of the divisions of formal psychology. The sportsperson who thinks he or she can discover a single authoritative and well-established body of knowledge about human nature betrays a naiveté. It is necessary to grasp the actual situation within psychology in order to proceed realistically. To compound matters, the diversity of backgrounds and interests of people in psychology is just about matched by that of people in sports. There are, then, realistic difficulties in bringing about useful interactions between psychology and sports. But hopefully there are few impossibilities.

Little Church Around the Couch

A concern about formal psychologies that many of us share is that they seem to add very little to what the shrewd and observing layman already knows about human behavior. This feeling occurs especially when we observe such a layman functioning in his occupation—for example, selling used cars or real estate. Many observers have the impression that psychologists tend to take a common-sense notion of behavior and then, through the application of statistical methods and mathematical models, either elaborate on the obvious or disguise it. Sometimes, it seems, the concept originally under consideration is even ignored as methodology becomes all-important.

But win, lose, or draw, fact or fancy, psychoanalysis has added something new and exciting to our views of human nature. The curbstone psychologists, whether ancient or modern, could not have come up with such a system of looking at our behavior. In fact, today's "common-sense psychologist" still does not know much about the analytic system and probably would not pay much attention to it even if he were informed. Remarkably, the same is true for many psychiatrists and psychologists.

A brief account of psychoanalysis cannot begin to do justice to this ingenious and imaginative system of perceiving human behavior. Its great value, it would seem to me, lies in its taking into account a number of key considerations that have been largely ignored by the academic psychologies.

1. Analysis places great emphasis on unconscious processes. Our philosophical heritage of the rational man was sharply and overwhelmingly challenged, and perhaps corrected, by the new views. Analysis drew attention to the underground mental processes that are highly influential in directing behavior. The case is so strong that it now seems remarkable that the unconscious was not given much attention prior to Freud. It is even more incredible that even now many psychologists attempt to give an account of human behavior without taking the unconscious into account. How can this be so? Both analysis and other psychologies may be at fault. In general, analysts, having a quasi-religious position, do not encourage outsiders to fool around with their beliefs. As for most of the scientific psychologists, they feel that considerations of the unconscious do not lend themselves to scientific methodologies. Such an attitude will not do for people who really want some answers about human behavior. Methodologies and systems that do not take account of a vital aspect of human behavior tend to be sterile academic exercises.

2. People have biographies. Prior to analysis no other system of psychology had ever paid attention to the obvious fact that people have or have had parents. This omission is rather made up for by the Freudian scheme. Biography, and especially very early biography, is regarded as being central to personality formation and subsequent behavior. The trouble is that under this system, while the parents play critical roles, there doesn't seem to be a formula that prescribes a way for them to be helpful. No matter how the parents behave they seem destined to injure the child's psyche.

3. The method of psychotherapy hit upon by analysis brought about powerful results, not all of them entirely benign. Freud first used hypnosis as a pipeline to the unconscious and then abandoned it in favor of a method that looks like free association. The patient was asked to say whatever came to mind and to include everything—even the apparently trivial. Anything might be revealing. The analyst was not the traditional kindly counselor who offered a compassionate pat on the back and wise advice on matters in the patient's life. There was no give-and-take dialogue. The burden was on the patient. The therapist did not offer quick and ready interpretations or solutions. In short, there were no discussions in the sense of normal dialogue as most of us understand it. Even more significant, normal emotional reactions on the part of the therapist were withheld. In contrast, if a patient were to make a hostile remark to another layman, he could expect a hostile reaction in return. But the therapist did not and still does not react like another layman. He might show no reaction, he might nod, or simply murmur "Hmm." The basic point is that during psychotherapy the patient undergoes an experience in which the normal responses of the world are altered or withheld. This experience turns out to be a powerful one that tends to produce a rollback or regression. It may set the stage for useful therapeutic correction or in some cases simply be dangerous—i.e., topple a patient into a psychosis.

The McGill University studies supply a startling backup to the pattern emerging from the analyst's couch. These studies suggest that we are dependent on normal reactions from the world for mental growth and sanity itself. If a dog is raised under excellent conditions of sanitation, nutrition, and exercise, but in an isolation that precludes normal stimulation or playback from the world, it becomes a very dumb dog. The experiments were continued, but they were obviously too cruel to inflict on dogs. Hence, college students were used as subjects. Increasingly, normal stimulation from the world was shut off. First, sound and sight. Then there was

an effort to eliminate tactile stimulation. The subject wore
long cuffs so that he could not feel anything except the inside
of the cuffs. The results were hair-raising. After a while, the
subject would go into a mental state resembling schizo-
phrenia, complete with full-blown hallucinations. A similar
phenomenon has been reported by adventurers who sail
alone across the oceans in small boats. There is often a
temporary loss of sanity. Sea monsters usually dominate the
hallucinations.

The person-to-person relationship in psychoanalytic
therapy is probably not as extreme as the non-stimulation
and non-playback seen either in the McGill experiments or in
the case of the isolated sailor. After all, the patient's contact
with the analyst occupies at most only a few hours each week.
The patient may have other important stimulations from his
environment. Our present goal is not to speculate on the
dangers of this kind of treatment for someone who is close to
the deep end. It is only to say that psychoanalysis hit upon a
most powerful pattern of human behavior.

4. *Sex.* For several generations most people who are even vaguely
familiar with Freud's reputation associate him with sex. His
system did indeed make sex an important factor in explaining
behavior. Other systems for the most part tried to avoid
sexual matters. Even religions have tried to avoid sex, but at
the same time giving it a central place. For most religions sex
has been a topic that is both hush-hush and yet at the very
core of morality; for some religions there would appear to be
little else. Thinking only "pure thoughts" puts you on the
road to heaven. The entertaining of "evil thoughts" puts you
on the road to hell. It is probably not as true any more, but a
youngster's natural biological drive and the stern warning of
a man of the cloth can bring about conflict and misery.

Freud regarded sex as one aspect of life that must be
given attention in any realistic account of human behavior. It
struck him that at the root of most of his patients' neurotic
problems there were sexual difficulties. His reports on the

importance of the sex drive in determining human behavior were met by icy reactions, especially from polite society in Vienna. Freud was apparently aghast at the cold reception his reports received. This coldness seemed to arouse the competitive spirit of a basically very tough competitor. As a result, part of Freud's effort may have become to emphasize sex further and find it in almost everything.

How important is the sex drive? It's difficult to compare basic drives. Experiments with animals indicate that sex is a rather minor drive in comparison with hunger or thirst. Yet society is so arranged that human beings seem to have much more difficulty handling the sex drive than other needs. Anyone who has general adjustment problems is likely to find the sexual adjustment a troublesome one. Hence, it may not be true that sexual adjustment, if bad, can cause all other maladjustments. Sexual adjustment may not be at the root. It may simply be the area in which general maladjustment breaks out most conspicuously.

5. *Dreams.* Some analysts think that Freud's greatest contribution was his theory of the interpretation of dreams. These baffling and strange adventures that we have while asleep were viewed by Freud as a significant approach to the unconscious. Freud's emphasis on the importance of dreams is mentioned here only as another aspect of a brilliant system. At present it's hard to see how the interpretation of dreams can form an important part of sports psychology. But who knows?

Psychoanalysis as a science / Analysis emerged from a medical setting. It came out of the effort to treat mental illness. It was not at all in the tradition of academic psychologies. In fact, psychoanalysis still pays no attention to what most psychologists are up to. They particularly ignore the animal experiments. For psychologists deciding whether an effort is scientific or not, the criteria usually applied are concerned with (1) communication, (2) experimentation, and (3) quantification. On all three counts psychoanalysis comes out in bad shape. The analysts do have a form of communication, but it is mostly with each other. Communication is generally intended for members only. Surely, there is little interest in communicating with the academic psychologists. There is no psychoanalytic experimentation in the sense known to most sciences. The data are anecdotal, whether written or presented at a case conference. Publications tend to relate to doctrine. At a case conference, the therapist reports to his colleagues and is responsible for both an account of his own behavior and that of the patient. Who can accept such testimony? As for quantification, there isn't any.

Analysis does ignore traditional psychology but the reverse isn't true. The insights into behavior that have come out of analysis are too rich and imaginative to be ignored. Analysis presents a gold mine of possible research projects. But there is a chasm between psychoanalysts and psychologists that is mostly a matter of methodology. The traditional psychologist wants to imitate the methods that have been so fruitful for the physical sciences. The analyst wants no part of such methods. Maybe he's right. It could be that "scientific methods" are not entirely appropriate for the study of human nature.

The psychologist confronts analysis / As we noted earlier, we don't know much about the motives that bring a student into the field of psychology. Motives must vary greatly. But it would seem to be a reasonable assumption that however subtle and indirect the sources there has to be an interest in human behavior. In some cases such an interest could derive from a special aptitude. A person may have a flair for understanding human behavior and want to further this ability by getting the benefits of scientific work in the field. As a graduate student, however, he is likely to be kept busy and distracted by statistics, mathematics, experiments with animals, specialized studies on vision. His interest can easily shift as a result of this interference from people to methods. Another type of graduate student has always been rather bewildered by human behavior. He may enter psychology with the hope that he can clear up his bewilderment. The great emphasis on methodologies "takes him off the hook," so to speak. He no longer need be concerned about understanding human behavior. He can devote himself to methodologies. He is now free of the mystery that has plagued him—the understanding of human behavior.

We can understand the psychologist a bit better if we turn our attention to his graduate training. Here is where the professional psychologist is created. Here is where the mold is cast. Naturally enough, faculty members teach in their own areas of interest and expertise. However, despite differences in subject orientation among universities, there does seem to be a common thread. The common thread is training in the scientific methods of the physical sciences. These methods include, among others, experimental design, rigorous methods of making inferences, and refinement of concepts. There is a premium on avoiding mentalism or any form of anthropomorphism even with respect to people.

Given the training, then, of an academic psychologist, is it any wonder that he does not embrace the doctrines of psychoanalysis? To him they seem ridiculously unscientific and perhaps amusing. What is most amusing appears to be the id, the ego, and the superego. The curious thing is that they appear to be three real characters. They can almost be pictured on the old vaudeville stage. All three wear baggy pants. The ego is in the middle, flanked by the id and the superego. Both the id and the superego have rolled-up newspapers and give the ego a pretty good swatting around. The ego is kind of a reasonable character. He wants to do the best he can to make things work out. He just wants to get along. But he is locked up in a partnership with unreasonable characters. The id selfishly screams, "I want gratification. Gratification! I don't care about the objective situation. Just give me what I want." The superego isn't a great deal of help to the unfortunate ego. The superego just reads the rule book and tells the ego that whatever it wants is not allowed. Suppose the ego wants to do a full day's work so that he can take care of the rent, food, and other obligations. The id might say insistently, "We want to go to the races." The dumb superego will say, "Gambling is evil." It's clear that neither of these characters is helpful to the ego. The job of the ego is to get along with his partners but still keep the upper hand so that he can get on about the business of coping with the world. I suppose some of us would have a little sympathy with the id. After all, we can't live forever and we do deserve some fun along the way. Even the superego might well attract the sympathies of some people, like clerics, old maids, and college deans. They too are obsessed with rules.

The psychologist tends to be a liberal person. He believes in giving a fair hearing to the views of others. You can tell about psychologists because many of them subscribe to *The New Yorker*, drive station wagons, and vote against all Republican candidates. The analysts can be viewed by psychologists as fellow liberals with whom one can work. After all, there is a common interest in scientific truth. Communication between the two disciplines should be easy. Interdisciplinary research would seem to be the key to discovering more about human behavior. All of us are so liberal that we might even invite a sociologist to join us. Why not meet for lunch regularly and discuss research approaches. We will meet in an affable setting, and it will be a great start toward cutting across disciplinary lines and producing some great research.

After the meetings have been under way for a while, the psychologist finds that the analyst does no homework. He doesn't prepare for the meetings. But then why should he? He already has a creed that supplies the answers. As one analyst expressed his position, "You have to eat lunch somewhere." It often takes the psychologist a long time to catch on to the idea that the analyst's notions of research are quite different from his own. The analyst has not the slightest intention of setting up research projects designed to test any of the basic tenets of his creed. Research of a kind is acceptable, but it has to show the unfolding of the analytic system in all of its glory and magnificence. No real examination of fundamental assumptions is invited. The poor psychologist might as well knock on the rectory door and say, "Father, I want to do research with you to test the existence of the Holy Ghost." The sociologist is not better off. He gets a polite hearing, but he makes no impact. The analyst believes that his methods work regardless of culture. A closed system does not borrow from outside. The sociologist believes that culture shapes behavior. For the analyst a university campus or the Sahara are all the same. After a while, the researchers begin to eat lunch in different places.

Psychoanalysis as a religion / It has already been suggested that analysis is a form of religion. But even if it is a religion, it still may be a valuable approach to understanding human behavior. Curiously, it may possibly offer much more than the "scientific systems." Like some other religions, analysis has an elaborate theology, one that can easily strain the credulity of the novice. He is put through a kind of test that includes a demonstration of faith. Before he is allowed to become a practicing priest, he must endure a rigorous and arduous training procedure that requires time and soul-searching. In many respects the training of the analyst is similar to that of the priest in the Catholic Church. In both instances the training sessions are like a small-meshed sieve. Making it through is not easy. The survivors tend to be reliable, stable people. The obstacles encountered in training are purposely difficult. Both psycho-analysis and the Catholic Church have a horror of letting themselves be represented by dummies or disturbed people. A certain number of disturbed people are acceptable in history, where they can be regarded as saints or pioneers. But at the present time it's not good to have too many upset people running loose. Ill-trained or disturbed personnel present a poor image and are dangerous to the stability and perpetuity of central structures.

Ernest Jones's account of Freud's life, surely one of the great biographies of all time, is in some ways a new testament or gospel. At many points the story is strikingly reminiscent of that of Christ and his apostles. Much of Christ's story was supposedly set down by his disciples. Jones was a most active and capable disciple of Freud. In reading Jones's three volumes you feel that you are present at the birth of a religion. You'll find biblical parallels even in Freud's continuing suspicion that a Judas was in his midst. He found at least two of them. Freud lived much longer than Christ—more than twice as long and in a much faster-moving age. After founding his church, he lived long enough to see his teachings spread to nearly all parts of the world. Though psychoanalysis had enormous impact on the intellectual world, there was opposition to its doctrines and, later on, those who practiced it were persecuted under the Nazis. But to Freud, even more disturbing than the opposition and persecution was the fact that apostates were founding new churches.

At staff meetings or case conferences of analytically oriented therapists there tends to be a church atmosphere. Nonmembers are not completely rejected, but they are really expected to be quiet and not disrupt the service in any way. When a training analyst is present, he is given great deference. When he makes a pronouncement, there is likely to be complete agreement with his views. His status appears to be like that of a bishop or, at the least, of a monsignor.

It appears that the analytic church draws most of its personnel from those who would have been inclined to be rabbis, priests, or ministers. Analysis seems to require a religious bent. Through many generations of severe hardships, the Jews have kept alive a love of scholarship, intellectualism, and a concern with religion. Psychoanalysis can be viewed as a product of Jewish genius and a devotion to particular values. So can Catholicism.

I happen to know three ex-altar boys who became analysts. Having given up one religion, they moved to another. Perhaps they found difficulty in accepting a system of doctrines that appeared to them either contradictory or naive. A religious impulse still stirred inside them, but a more sophisticated religion was needed. Enough of such myths as the Garden of Eden. Yet, in changing over, other myths had to be dealt with, like the story of the unfortunate Oedipus, who got trapped in an unusual situation. In general, however, the intellectual apostate Catholics are not likely candidates for analysis. Extricating themselves from the Catholic Church was probably a painful experience. They don't covet the opportunity to go through it again with another religion.

To know only that a person is a Protestant doesn't tell

you much about him. He might be anyone from the archbishop of Canterbury to a bible school graduate preaching hellfire in the rural areas. The most productive source of Protestants who might serve the analytic cause can probably be narrowed down to the better divinity schools. These schools seem to assemble groups of sensitive students who want to be of service to mankind but don't know quite how to go about it. It's not unusual for a divinity student to transfer to a school of social work that is oriented toward analytic psychiatry. However, upon completion of his training he seems destined to occupy a rough spot. He is bound to remain a low man on the totem pole. The M.D. is the prestige guy, mostly because he can wave his medical cloak. The Ph.D. is next in line because he can rightfully demand to be called "Doctor," though he may have to keep reminding people of his title. The social worker will have the least prestige, the lowest salary, and the most personal insecurity. The old image of the social worker as someone who brings a basket of food to the needy remains to plague him. One chief psychiatrist told me that he considered his social workers to be his best therapists, but the system prevented him from rewarding them properly.

FREUD'S GREAT APOSTATE
Freud's great apostate was Alfred Adler, though some readers might, with some justification, think of Carl Jung as having made the more significant contributions to psychology. We use the term "apostate" in talking about Adler with some hesitancy because Adler's "individual psychology" would not appear to be a complete break with analysis. However, Freud thought it was and never forgave Adler. When Freud, who was living his last days in England after escaping from the Nazis, received the news of Adler's

death, there was no sorrow in his reaction—in fact, there was almost a rejoicing.

Adler had almost everyone using the phrase "inferiority complex." He believed that the mainspring of human behavior is a feeling of inferiority. Such a feeling could derive either from a physical deficiency or from something imagined, but it is always there. The key to personality and behavior is the way the inferiority feeling is handled. One's behavior in reacting to his feelings of inferiority determines his "life-style." The behavior can run the range all the way from direct onslaught on the inferiority to other achievements or to a "fictive goal." The "fictive goal" is a kind of escape. It amounts to self-pity and is no real achievement. Almost every athletic coach has had to cope with the "fictive goal" pattern.

The compensation for an inferiority can be direct. Examples of this kind of reaction are striking when they do occur. Demosthenes, the legendary Greek orator, overcame a speech defect by practicing speeches with pebbles in his mouth at the seashore, where he challenged himself to declaim loud enough to be heard above the noise of the surf. Theodore Roosevelt was a frail and sickly youngster. Nature had shortchanged him. But Roosevelt reacted to his deficiency by deciding that he was going to build his body, and he became a physically powerful man. A little more than a generation ago the mile run in the United States was dominated by five great runners. These five great performers had one curious thing in common. When they were youngsters each was in danger of losing a leg through disease or accident. Each of these athletes made an effort to compensate directly and the result was great achievement. A single case of such a pattern would have been startling enough. But five out of five of the top milers seems to defy credibility! Yet, it did happen. Similar cases exist. A youngster with a deformed arm decided to become a hammer thrower. Because this event requires great strength, his goal seemed to be impossible. Incredibly, he eventually not only won the Olympic championship but also broke the world record.

Direct compensation for a physical inferiority is both dramatic and admirable, but we can't expect it to happen too often. From the standpoint of athletic achievement the best bet might be the highly gifted athlete with a strong inferiority feeling about his athletic ability. In other words, a biological billionaire who feels like a pauper. His feelings could supply the drive that would enable him to use his great assets. Such a pattern could well be one of the secrets of enormous athletic performance.

Do inferiority feelings make the academic world go round? / It is a curious bit of Americana that our academic institutions are the hub of amateur athletics and the cradle of professional athletics. The relationship between athletics and academia has never been adequately dealt with. The athletic director may give talks about the essential part athletics play in education and then hire a coach who will never be able to locate any campus building other than the gym. There have been prominent athletes who could neither read nor write. As for the top administrators, such as the presidents and deans, they have to tread lightly. After all, athletic competition is better than duels or riots. And good teams are important to fund raising.

The sensitive coach has to entertain some inferiority feelings of his own and question the value of his functions in comparison with those of the academic faculty. The aware coach recognizes that the academicians execute the basic function at a university. At times he may have the gnawing suspicion that the coaches conduct an irrelevant sideshow that only detracts from the events of the main tent.

The professors also have their inferiority feelings. The typical faculty member has had an excellent grade record in both college and graduate school. But much of his record may be a result of drive supplied by inferiority feelings. Of course, he had to have enough innate ability to carry him over the academic obstacle course. Like the athlete, he tends to slow down if his inferiority feelings diminish along the way. In terms of his achievement, it would be better to keep him running, give him no peace, give him no rest. But the academician does get a brief respite when he receives his Ph.D. The degree is a kind of certification: "You are a scholar and an intellectual, and here is the paper to prove it."

But the rest period afforded the Ph.D. degree is short-lived. As a young faculty member, his ability to teach isn't all that critical. However, he must publish. His early publications appear in the various journals. Lectures accumulate and are refined until there are enough of them for a hardcover book. It makes very little difference if anybody reads the book. Its existence should bring tenure for the young writer. Once tenure has been gained, there is no longer a need to run or think. Does this seem an unlikely account?

The productivity of academicians, as measured by the number of their publications, has been tabulated with reference to age: it was found that after they reached their early thirties, their output declined. The peak is passed and there is a sharp decline. Just as he is reaching a position in which his increased maturity and learning should lead to enormous and significant productivity, the academician sluffs off. Why should such a peculiar and discouraging pattern exist? It's largely because the inferiority complex has been negated, and there is little need to run any more. There is time to attend faculty teas now, and to serve on faculty committees. He can now become "delightful" and a "person of stature."

Life-style / The Adlerian view, as noted, assumes that all of us have or have had strong feelings of inferiority. There need not be an actual physical defect or weakness. The feelings are there anyway, probably because everyone in his infancy was in a helpless and weak state. If we assume that basic inferiority feelings always exist, the critical matter becomes how they are handled—or what "life-style" is adopted.

An outstanding mental hygiene clinic at a large university became interested in what groups made use of the clinic's facilities. Through the use of computers students were grouped according to categories such as academic standing, course of study, religion, activities. The only group that tended not to use the clinic were those students who participated in intercollegiate athletics. Inferences are difficult to make, but this survey at least suggests that successful athletic activity is related to personal adjustment.

Life-style and athletics / The person whose goals are predominantly "fictive" is engaged in an effort, probably for the most part unconscious, to avoid a direct and realistic approach to life's problems. He makes an effort to fool himself and others. And there can often be a kind of temporary success, but the price is paid in terms of personal neurosis. There may be areas in which a "fictive" life-style can produce gratifying results—i.e., getting sympathy from other people. But it doesn't work in sports.

The "fictive" life-style is often seen in sports but is not rewarded well. All coaches hear from some athletes the constant recital of adversities that stand in the way of their recording achievement in sport. Laments over illness, injuries, studies, problems at home, and more are familiar to the coach. The coach can sometimes be taken in, but the event never is. The event has no sympathy at all. It represents stark reality. For example, a discus knows nothing and cares nothing about beautifully articulated accounts of personal difficulties. The distance that the discus goes depends only upon the athlete's ability to perform. An athletic event makes no adjustment to the athlete. The adjustment is all his. It is strictly reality testing.

Life-style and age / Adler felt that life-style is established in childhood. The concrete hardens quickly, and after that no significant changes in life-style can be expected. We can hope that Adler was a bit wrong in his view that life-style is established early and never again is subject to real change. After all, we do seem to see some people change some of their behavior patterns as they mature. But all in all it would seem likely that the younger a person is, the easier it is to effect a change in him.

The task of "character building" probably falls much more to the high school coach than to the college coach. The main reason for this, of course, is that the high school coach's subjects are younger and presumably more pliable. Life-style can be more readily changed. Second, the members of a university team are survivors. The youngsters who are candidates for college teams have already passed a certain amount of reality testing. Many with "fictive" life-styles have already been eliminated. Those who have failed to meet the test are no longer around—except for a few who have extraordinary physical gifts. Regardless of his psychological makeup, a great physical specimen cannot be easily dismissed. Suppose a football candidate weighs

230 pounds and has been clocked in 9.4 seconds for the hundred yards. Even if this athlete's life-style suggests that he will never come through with reliable performances, the potential is so great that it is not easy for the coach to give up on him. The coach will try, desperately at times, to change the athlete's life-style. The coach can't believe what he sees. The odds for the coach are bad. The candidate is likely to remain a problem athlete, a carrot dangled tantalizingly before the coach's nose.

What should the high school coach do? / The age factor is important in changing life-styles. It seems that the older the subject, the less the chance of changing him. Thus, the high school coach has a better chance of changing the life-styles of athletes than does the college coach. The high school coach will be dealing with a great range of life-styles. At one happy extreme, he will be dealing with youngsters who already have the life-style needed for effective athletic performance. At the other extreme, there will be youngsters who, despite having enough physical ability, have life-styles that interfere with sports achievement. It is between the extremes that the coach may have his best chance to accomplish something of great significance to the future of a youth.

The dedicated coach would like to help the youngster who has a nonproductive life-style. But, unfortunately, there is no simple formula available to the coach. No formula—only suggestions. And any offering of suggestions recognizes that the coach must rely mostly on his artistry as a teacher. But the coach can get some help from the field of psychology. He can be made aware that an athlete may be presenting a life-style that needs changing. A coach's virtues—his patience, insight, and effort—might be rewarded by winning seasons, but there is a greater reward in helping his subjects establish a new pattern of behavior that could relieve some of the potential misery that may occur in the long life that the youth has before him.

The coach deals with a life-style that has existed for rather a long time—presumably since the athlete's childhood. The coaching approach has to be sensitive, as the coach moves between Scylla and Charybdis. It takes a bit of doing and timing. And sympathy too. But the sympathy has to lie with the athlete and not with the specific difficulties that he brings up. The coach cannot be useful to the athlete if he allows himself to be taken in by the life-style. The coach should represent reality. He should constantly emphasize the realities presented by the sports event itself. He should get across the idea that "It's too bad you have so many problems, but here is what success in the event requires." The coach definitely should not take the position of "You are yellow. Shape up or get off the squad." The athlete with a disqualifying life-style is not "yellow." He has a problem that abrupt and grotesque handling will not solve.

Because the athlete's self-negating life-style has existed for a long time, a weaning process is probably necessary. As suggested, the role of the coach is far from easy. To bring about real changes in personality structure the coach has to be an extraordinary teacher. In his efforts to change life-style the coach has one great ally—the athletic event itself. The coach can bring about a constant direction to the event and what it requires. The event never adjusts to the athlete; rather, the athlete must do all the adjusting, which is good reality training. The athlete may, because of his life-style, tell the coach not to expect much of him because "I'm weak and ill and my muscles are sore." The coach can respond, "You do seem to have problems, but I know you'll do the best that you can." This dialogue or something like it may be repeated often, but there is the chance that the athlete's "best" will become better. He might even turn in a world record performance.

Using the revelations of the couch / There is a strong suggestion that at least for the present the "scientific," or academic, psychologies are not the ones that are most likely to offer us the most help in understanding human nature. At present the "depth" psychologies, of which psychoanalysis is one, seem to offer the most to coaches and others interested in human behavior. In other parts of this book I will be drawing on the findings of the couch. The findings are signficant. Some analysts (maybe most or even all) will be upset by my belief that their "science" has strong religious overtones. Though "depth" psychologies do have roots in medical practice, I think they also have religious aspects. And is there anything wrong with all of that? Under the present state of the art, such a religous approach might well be the most useful of the various psychological efforts. The religious aspects in themselves may not be entirely harmful. The main difficulty is that communication becomes impeded under this approach. Ideas become confined to the priesthood. On television quiz programs the Bible is frequently a topic for questions. The average Catholic would be badly defeated by the average Protestant on such a show. It's because the Catholic priesthood has traditionally controlled and kept semi-secret the Bible as an esoteric document not intended for the scrutiny of the uninitiated. In contrast, the Protestant sects, which are offshoots of Catholicism, encourage Bible reading. Now, as we try to make use of the significant findings of analysis, could it be that the offshoots of the basic church of analysis, such as the Adlerian group, would be more willing to let us in on things?

It seems to be the curious pattern that a significant bit of knowledge about human behavior tends to be staked out as private property by a cultist group. The group may represent itself as a science or as a religion. For example, sociometry, presumably a science, has some fascinating and important methods of dealing with the relationships of an individual to his fellows. But their methods are covered by a baffling veneer of esoteric views. A formal religion can be built around a significant aspect of human behavior. For example, the remarkable phenomenon of suggestibility supplies the base for Christian Science.

The eclectic who pursues an interest in human behavior is often compelled, in a sense, to peer through picket fences. He is not encouraged to study, use, or even comment on the views of a cult. The eclectic is not welcomed unless he appears to be a potentially desirable convert. The analyst takes the position that the eclectic cannot understand psychoanalysis without being analyzed. But being analyzed, even if the idea is found acceptable, involves a profound commitment including much time and money. For the eclectic observer the demands of membership in the psychoanalytic cult seem unreasonable. Consider how many cults there are where similar demands are made. After all, how many years are there in a lifetime? Even if you could go from one cult to another, the last cult you left would take the position that you never really understood its teachings. A sensible position to be adopted is the following: "We are interested in whatever valuable contributions your group may be able to make to our understanding of human nature. We would like to share in this knowledge without incurring the obligations of full membership."

Ask the Animals

We have to talk about the animals. The coach and the athlete are especially concerned with motor learning. Increased proficiency in mastering techniques in athletic events obviously depends on the discovery and development of more effective learning processes. It is natural enough for the coaches to turn toward the learning theories of psychology in their search for help—for the elusive "edge." However, it is sobering to know that most major learning theories are based on observations of animal behavior made in the laboratory—that is, under artificial conditions.

One of the early premises of experimentation with animals was that no sharp line existed between the behavior of infrahumans and that of humans. Such a premise would leave us free to extrapolate from the findings. The principles that applied to animal behavior would to some degree and in some senses apply also to human behavior. There would surely seem to be some common core in that most creatures, like man, have a nervous system and the task of mediating the environment. Nevertheless, if we fail to distinguish between animals and human beings we can get into difficulties.

Animals are not simplified replicas of mankind. Anyone who has ever raised a pet animal knows this to be true. A rapport exists between owner and animal. They understand each other in a way that laboratory experimentation cannot measure. We are not talking just about an eccentric old woman, for example, who has willed a fortune to her pet. Not all people who seem anthropomorphic about animals are naive. For example, Freud was entirely convinced that he had a deep and subtle relationship with his pet chow. Later on, a pet female dog he owned escaped and had an affair with a poodle reputed to be a splendid specimen. Freud reported that though the dog experienced no real pregnancy, it did have a curious "false pregnancy."

DARWIN AND THORNDIKE

In 1859 Charles Darwin published *On the Origin of Species*. The world hasn't been the same since. The influence of this publication and others that followed hardly needs comment. Obviously, biology was revolutionized. But the book's effects were also strongly felt in religion, philosophy, literature, and, of course, psychology. It seems doubtful that Darwin had a real inkling of the earthshaking impact his work was to have. He did a great deal of legwork, but his writing was basically reportorial. However, his brilliant defender, Thomas Huxley, perceived the implications of Darwin's findings. Huxley clearly anticipated both the hostile rejection of Darwin's theories by society and the fierce struggle that would be needed to convince the world of the plausibility of the theory of evolution. He relentlessly employed his great talents and energies in support of Darwinism.

Bridging the gap—The anecdotal period / Our concern is with the effects that Darwinism produced on psychology. Before Darwin only human beings were considered appropriate subjects for psychological study. Animals were thought to have no mental processes, only instincts. But now the Darwinian view theorized a continuity in mental functioning between the infrahumans and man. The animals certainly should have been upgraded, but the view of continuity in mental processes has led to some peculiar and misleading results.

The theory of psychological continuity in a way made all creatures brothers and sisters under the skin, scales, fur, or feathers. Since this was assumed to be so, all we had to do was to observe the animals correctly and we would see that they are capable of doing nearly everything that humans can do. We then had the anecdotal period. Remarkable mental feats by animals were reported. There was one long and colorful report of crows holding a trial by jury. A truly unusual performance when you consider that trial by jury only gradually entered the British system of jurisprudence and is still unknown in many parts of the world. The report failed to specify the types of cases tried by the crows. We can only assume that they were both criminal and civil. Some of us may think there is nothing more disgusting than a crooked crow. But really, what could a bad crow do? Steal a little corn maybe? But such an act would hardly single him out among his peers. Which of them can claim to have clean beaks! Of course, the whole notion of crows trying each other by jury does seem ridiculous. Yet there is one disquieting fact. Some crows can talk! To hear one is an unforgettable experience.

I don't recall a crow saying anything that would be quotable at a cocktail party. A constant repetition of "My name is Joe the crow" would probably not enlighten most discussions. But under oath, who knows? Might we hear, "To the best of my recollection, Senator . . ."?

End of the anecdotal period / Eventually psychologists began to lose faith in the mental prowess of the animals. Perhaps the anecdotes became too extravagant. At any rate the whole effort came to be regarded as a dead end. The pendulum had swung full. The thinking apparently went somewhat as follows: We've tried promoting the animals; that didn't do much good. The animals let us down. All right then, if promotion does not do any good, let's try demotion. Let's treat the animals like dummies and see if that gets us anywhere.

It was in 1896 that the animals were first stripped of their dignity and status. They were taken into the laboratory and placed in trick cages called "puzzle boxes." Various animals were used, though cats seemed to bear the brunt of the work. A typical experiment was one in which a hungry cat was placed in a cage with food in sight outside the cage. The cat seemed to have two motivations. First, he didn't like being cooped up in the cage. Second, he was hungry and wanted the food that he could see and not get to. Being rather desperate, he would claw and bite nearly everything he could contact. Sooner or later, he would hit the latch and open the cage door. With enough repetitions of the experiment the cat would go directly to the latch and open the door.

Thorndike, the most prominent puzzle box experimenter, attributed no powers of reasoning or insight to the cats. It was entirely a matter of trial and error. But in explaining the stamping-in of the response that opened the cage, Thorndike fell back on what he called the "law of effect." The effective action was stamped in because it was satisfying and pleasurable. Such a law was not at all satisfactory to his successors, who considered it anthropomorphic and a regression to the anecdotal method.

In early experiments Thorndike worked with newly hatched chicks. If he placed one on a low box it would jump off. If he placed one on a box a few inches high the chick would jump, but only after some hesitation. When the box was a foot high, the chick wouldn't jump at all. This pattern should have given the experimenter pause about a strictly trial-and-error theory of behavior.

By tradition the animal experimenters are "objective" and quantitative in reporting behavior. Such a methodology does not give a full account of what the animal does. For example, the cat always made it clear that he did not find the puzzle box activities congenial. He would often attack the experimenter. Even Thorndike himself once had a rough time subduing one of the larger cats who went after him. Anyone who has ever worked with cats knows that they are not automatons. They often display independence and temperament.

Thorndike still entertained a slight doubt about his theoretical position. There was a lingering possibility that animals might, after all, reason. But he considered this doubt put to rest by an experiment in which animals that had learned a particular trick performed for animals that had not. The ignorant animals didn't get a thing out of watching the animals that already knew their stuff. A harsh experiment! Would we like to judge the mentality of students by what they get out of watching the coaches and faculty? But as a matter of fact it has been established that apes can indeed learn via imitation.

BEHAVIORISM

Behaviorism, a school within psychology, began as a rebellion against traditional psychology. The great psychologists had maintained that psychology should be concerned only with conscious experience. Work with animals was useful only to the extent that it could shed light on the consciousness of human beings. Not entirely a bad position! After all, medical research with animals must finally relate to human beings. For example, the eventual goal of cancer research with mice cannot be to cure these creatures of cancer. Who would contribute to that?

Behaviorism emerged as both a protest and a methodology. The protest was mostly against the use of literary and religious concepts that threatened to finish off psychology as a science. The methodology was to concentrate entirely on reports of behavior. Both the stimulus situation and behavior were to be controlled and specified. Quantification became important. It was hoped that if these things were done, psychology could free itself from philosophy, religion, and literature and in this way become a true science. The traditionalists' response was that such methodology may make for a science. But a science of what? Surely not psychology.

Pavlov and the conditioned reflex / The revolt toward behaviorism was already well under way before Pavlov's work in Russia became known in America. But Pavlov's findings were greeted by the behaviorists. They surely seemed to fill the bill. The behaviorists now had a base to work with. Pavlov was a physiologist with an interest in the digestive process. In his work with dogs he collected their saliva. He presented food to get the dogs to salivate. But he noticed that the dogs salivated before the food actually got there. They anticipated the food. They picked up clues.

Pavlov found this pattern to be of enormous significance and set up elaborate experiments to study it. Wouldn't a lot of us say that it would have been better for Pavlov to have taken the "common sense" route? He did not. But remember that his first serious study was for the priesthood.

We know that the relationship between man and dog goes back many, many thousands of years. Cave drawings attest to the existence of the relationship throughout antiquity. The dog was a junior partner in the hunt, and he expected to be fed. We know that a hungry dog wants to eat and expects to eat. So do we, and that's why we should be understanding. For nearly every creature salivation takes place upon the perception of food, or even its expectation. The salivation is a preparation for adequate digestion. Pavlov called this natural reaction to the food an unconditioned reflex. From his earlier observations he already knew that the dog could pick up clues to when the food was really coming along. But to make his method more specific Pavlov introduced a number of signals, including bells and buzzers. Almost anything would have done the job. If the signal appeared followed by the food a number of times, the dog would salivate upon the presentation of the signal alone. This pattern was called conditioning. But the dog could not be fooled for long. If the food stopped following the signal, the dog eventually ignored the signal. He no longer salivated. The failure to respond to a signal was called "extinction." The pattern of conditioning and extinction was regarded as Copernican. It was seized upon by behaviorists and others as the building block for a truly scientific psychology. At last there seemed to be a method of getting rid of literary and religious concepts in explaining human behavior.

How solid a base is the Pavlovian conditioned reflex

for building a theory of human nature? When a graduate student thinks that he has established a conditioned reflex in a laboratory animal, it becomes almost an occasion for a celebration. Surely the graduate student who works with animals has come to realize that conditioned reflexes are hard to effect, and even if established, quickly fade away.

A pet dog knows when he is going to be fed. He responds to any number of clues: the clattering of his dish, the opening of the can of food, the putting down of newspapers. If he is really hungry, any clue will bring about a frenzy of anticipation in the animal. But if any pet owner were cruel enough to go through the preliminary motions of feeding the animal, and then withhold the food, the anticipatory responses of the animal would soon be extinguished. He would find out that the deal isn't on the level.

The basic conditioned-reflex experiment of Pavlov has been repeated by thousands of psychologists and students in all parts of the world. There are variations and elaborations, and the laboratory equipment has become more sophisticated. The basic conditioning method that started with salivation has been applied to a variety of possible responses—for example, withdrawal of the animal's paw upon application of electric shock. But the pattern has remained similar. The animal is given clues that with repetition can help him to anticipate the stimulus that is to come. But when only the clues continue and the stimuli are stopped, anticipatory responses cease. In considering Pavlovian conditioning as the building block for our theories of behavior the great difficulty is the phenomenon of extinction. Conditioning is not stable. The conditioned reflex is not permanent. How can we build a theory of human behavior around it?

Nevertheless, when Pavlov's work became known in

America, it had tremendous impact. Some psychologists thought that the whole answer to human behavior had been revealed. We could do away with literary and religious ideas because we were simply a mass of conditioned reflexes touched off by one stimulus after another. Unfortunately, in the initial enthusiasm not enough attention was paid to the instability of the conditioned response.

The behaviorists thought psychology could progress only by dealing with behavior that could be observed and quantified. But there was a "missing link," and this seemed to be supplied by Pavlov's findings. The need of the behaviorists was so great that Pavlovianism was accepted without the critical scrutiny that would normally be applied. Watson, the colorful leader of the behaviorist movement in America, believed that through conditioning the biographies and personalities of human beings could be completely controlled. As a result of conditioning, a child could become anything from a criminal to a saint.

What we have said, I think, suggests that Pavlovian conditioning, which once gave impetus to behaviorism, is really no longer needed by the behaviorists. Yet even now some people still live by the old conditioned reflex. A few years ago, the Yale athletic coaches were assembled to hear an address by an expert on sports psychology. He was brought to the United States from Portugal under the auspices of our Department of State. The plan was for him to go from one university to another, spreading his gospel of psychology among American coaches. The advance notice credited him with being fluent in English. He began his talk by saying that the conditioned reflex, as set forth by Pavlov, supplies a complete account of sports psychology. As coaches, he said, all we had to do was understand the conditioning process and apply it to our athletes. To me this premise did not promise to be a good use of our time. Hence, I raised my hand and suggested that a strictly Pavlovian approach toward education had in this country been discarded for more than a generation. I expressed the hope that our approach to sports psychology could prove more fruitful for the meeting. I would have been kinder, but I had no idea that he had a canned talk on Pavlov and that it was almost the complete extent not only of his "fluent English" but of his knowledge of psychology and coaching as well. The chap had a rough idea that I was threatening him with trouble, but the translator had to go over my remarks a few times. After that, there wasn't much of a meeting. After his departure, the lecturer wrote to Yale several times, singling me out as "that fellow" and promising to supply proof that I was wrong. The "proof" never arrived. I would have been interested in seeing it. It was clear that he felt somewhat hostile toward me, and I can understand why. As for me, I just hope he will stop. I have no other hostile feelings and even hope that he is doing something useful. Portugal has a fine climate for growing grapes.

A "new type of conditioning" / In 1938 *The Behavior of Organisms* was published by B. F. Skinner. This book too had impact: it was a highly sophisticated and scholarly publication. In all fairness I must pause to say that I am a bit prejudiced in favor of Skinner. When I was a graduate student at Columbia I had a correspondence with Skinner, who was then at Minnesota. He was most helpful in advising me on the research program that I was trying to conduct. Surely Skinner is a genius. Nevertheless, I don't feel we can afford to be dazzled by brilliance. We have to plod along in the best way we can. A reasonably intelligent layman, if he could find his way through Skinner's writings, might find it puzzling that such a shining mentality put out such efforts to do away with the concept of mentality.

A distinction between "instrumental" and Skinner's "operant" conditioning is vital to an understanding of what the animal psychologists have been doing—and of the significance for extrapolation to human behavior. Pavlov's type of conditioned reflex is called "instrumental." In the Pavlovian method the response is elicited. The food elicits salivation, and then the dog's response is hooked up to an anticipatory signal such as a bell. In "operant" conditioning the animal first emits behavior—i.e., he does something. A segment of the animal's behavior is selected by the experimenter for "reinforcement," or stamping in. Of course, the reverse could be true, and the experimental effort might be to stamp out. But the stamping-in comes first.

Reinforcement implies a reward—a delight, a satisfaction. In operant conditioning, when an animal chances on a bit of behavior that the experimenter wants him to learn, that behavior is reinforced by a reward, usually food or water. That means that the experimenter must be sure that the animal is either hungry or thirsty to begin with. If it is not, conditioning is difficult.

The emitted response to be reinforced can be almost anything in the animal's repertory of possible actions. A pigeon may simply raise its head, and the raising of the head can be reinforced. Much more complicated combinations can be reinforced; pigeons can even be taught to play a form of Ping-Pong. But from the experimenter's point of view pressing a bar seems to be the best kind of response to reinforce and measure. Rats are very suitable for bar pressing. When confined to a box with a bar, the rats will get around to pressing it. And when the pressing of the bar yields food and drink, the pressing becomes frantic.

The basic method of "operant conditioning" is highly effective, even startling. And it has been for a long time. Animal trainers have been using a similar method for generations. All circus-goers know the remarkable things that can be taught to lions, tigers, and elephants. I suppose we are less impressed by the training of elephants than by that of the wild cats. Though they can be very tough at times, we tend to regard elephants as friendly, useful creatures who give rides to children on their backs and help by carrying logs and performing other useful chores. But lions and tigers don't do anything to help us. They have to be regarded as absolute battlers and menaces. With a single swing of a paw they can easily crush a human skull. When an animal trainer enters a cage with lions and tigers, he must have more than a statistical edge. He can't really afford a bad day. Every creature in the cage with him is a potential killer. His training methods have to work—or else! From all reports "operant conditioning" seems to be central to the training of lions and tigers. But there must be some variation in method. During an experiment with white rats, the psychologist wants them hungry. The same could possibly be true of the animal trainer, but keeping the lions and tigers too hungry could introduce a note of uneasiness.

CONDITIONING AND COACHING

"Instrumental" / It's hard to believe that the Pavlovian conditioning pattern, because it is so lacking in stability, can form a cornerstone of athletic coaching. Is it really so extraordinary that a dog can be fooled for a while by a buzzer or bell into thinking that he's going to get some food? It would seem that putting the dog's anticipatory reactions into a framework of conditioning, in an effort to avoid the horrors of anthropomorphism, does violence to the animal's mentality. I have been reading about Pavlov's work with dogs off and on for decades, and I still don't think it remarkable or particularly useful. Of course, I have to be impressed by the great stir that has been created. Thousands of psychologists have staked their careers on Pavlovian conditioning, and millions of people had their thinking influenced by it. Still and all, I don't see how this type of conditioning can be applied to coaching problems.

"Operant" / The results of operant conditioning are much more dramatic and solid than those of instrumental conditioning. However, in operant conditioning much of the experimental work involves white rats performing in a Skinner box. In the Skinner box the only activity of the animal that breaks into the record is lever pressing.

Suppose a brilliant person like Einstein could be placed in a Skinner box. His repertory of possible responses would be reduced to one: pressing a bar when he was hungry or thirsty. Einstein would have to be reported solely on the basis of his lever pressing. On such a basis we would know hardly anything about him. We know that he didn't spend all of his time and talents trying to get food pellets and water.

Skinner believes—and has pushed the idea in a major book—that operant conditioning can and should bring about a new society. If his method of conditioning promises to be that powerful, it would seem that it should be useful to the coach and athlete. But in considering the application of operant conditioning to the coaching situation we have to take account of two important considerations. First, there is the fact of human neuroses. Not all people want their responses to lead to pleasure. The behavior of such people is often not amenable to the normal laws of learning. Reinforcement under these conditions becomes difficult. In a later section we will be taking a closer look at this pattern.

Second, we must examine the realities of athletic events. In an athletic performance various acts occur in sequence, and they must blend together to be effective. As an example, let's consider the pole vault, a spectacular event familiar to most of us. In performing, the vaulter carries the pole, runs, plants the pole, takes off, lies back on the pole, etc. For the purpose of looking at the coaching situation we can abstract a series of acts—a,b,c, . . . n. Any one act in the sequence can be carried out only if the previous act is well carried out. The physical reality is that b can't be performed well unless a is all right, and c has no chance of succeeding unless b is good. And so it goes.

How does conditioning literature help the coach and the athlete? It's hard to see a direct connection. Let's go back to our sequence of a . . . n. The experienced coach knows that any one act in the sequence, call it e, can be a stumbling block. A poor performance of e precludes the effectiveness of acts that happen after e. If we can make e right, we are confident that the athlete can improve his performance substantially. But how can conditioning help us? One trouble is that e may blend into f in less than a tenth of a second. It becomes difficult to isolate e in time for possible reinforcement. Further, we usually don't know what is reinforcing to the athlete. Could it be an encouraging word from the coach? Possibly, at the high school level. Again, it should be emphasized that the sequence of acts represents the reality of athletic performance. The ability to perform an act effectively depends on how well the acts leading up to it have been carried out. A single poorly performed act can destroy the effectiveness of the subsequent acts. If the coach can successfully correct imperfect critical single acts he is going to have the "edge" that he usually seeks.

In the series of acts a critical act can be very brief and be quickly followed by another act. For example, in the high jump the most critical act takes place on the last stride toward the crossbar. For the jump to be successful the athlete must use the last stride to obtain a good lift, or takeoff. The average athlete is "pulled" to the crossbar. The critical act of takeoff becomes ineffective. The next act, the actual clearing of the bar, cannot be well executed. Then, coach and athlete may continue to work on clearance of the crossbar until they are both completely frustrated. There will be no efficient clearance until the preceding act is sound. If the coach had a way of reinforcing the critical act of takeoff, there would be a dramatic improvement in jumping performance. In fact, almost any able-bodied youngster would learn to jump rather well. At present, there doesn't seem to be any way for coaches to make use of Skinner's findings. All that they seem to be able to do is to keep directing the athlete's attention to the connection between the critical act of takeoff and the final performance. But then the process is no longer strictly one of conditioning.

In a way the law of effect has to be considered a sort of conditioning phenomenon. In a typical experiment of Thorndike the cat makes a response that frees him from the cage. The behaviorists really can't accept the mental implications of the law of effect—i.e., the cat gets "pleasure" in escaping from the puzzle box. As for me, I have no objection to the notion that the cat feels pretty good about getting free. My objection is that the cat's behavior has little or no application to the coaching situation. In the puzzle box there is no real series of *a* to *n*.

GIVE THE ANIMALS A BETTER CHANCE

The maze / The first known maze in modern times was designed for human beings. To amuse himself and his guests, an English aristocrat planted hedges in such a way that they formed twisting, winding pathways, false exits, and dead ends. The maze thus formed had an entrance and an exit, but between them there were lots of confusing, perplexing turns and convolutions. The task of getting from the entrance to the exit seemed severe and even overwhelming to some people.

If the maze could put humans to a test, psychologists thought, why not use it for the animals? Mazes were constructed especially for rats. This development gave rise to thousands of experiments and thousands of publications in the journals. The idea, at first, was that by observing the rats in the maze we could learn something that could meaningfully be applied to human behavior. Unfortunately, however, most behavior of the rat in the maze has been reported within the framework of a kind of behaviorism—that is, in terms of stimulus and response. The rat was viewed as learning each separate choice in the maze and then stringing these learned acts together to get through the entire maze.

The maze, when used for experimentation with animals, surely was an ingenious device, but one gets the feeling that it could have been better used to advance our understanding of behavior. That this was not true may be the fault both of our system of graduate training and of the editors of the journals. Neither the instructors nor the editors dared to appear anthropomorphic. Only quantification was tolerated. The rat's behavior had to be boiled down to numbers. Such a process omitted much rich observational material. Anyone who has ever run rats in a maze knows that the rats "learn the maze." They do not operate on a simple stimulus-and-response basis.

If similar conditions in a maze could be arranged for a man and a white rat, which would do better? In such a strange competition the rat would win. The point is that if we view the infrahumans as inferior replicas of human beings, we are accepting a harmful premise. Each species has had its own evolutionary pattern. As a result they are different from us. They are inferior to us in some spectacular ways, but they are superior in others.

A fair look at the rat running the maze shows that the rat's orientation is remarkable. A human being does not gain this degree of orientation in most life situations. The rat's unusual orientation is shared by many other animals. The condominium in which I live is in a string of others with common walls. It has a front door and two rear doors. Because of the arrangement if you leave by the front door and want to reenter by a rear door you have to walk around the block. The newsboys and delivery people are constantly confused in trying to correlate the front and back doors. But when I feed a stray cat, it has no confusion about the door. If it fails to get attention at a rear door, it will swing around the block and come quickly and directly to the front door.

The migrational habits of birds and fish ought to give pause to those who are obsessed with stimulus and response. The homing pigeon is one astonishing example. When released far from home, even hundreds of miles, it is able to get back to where it came from. Can the average psychologist perform such a feat? Eventually he'd make it but he would probably have to stop every so often to ask directions of a cop or a gas station attendant.

The apes get their chance / Most psychologists get very little opportunity to monkey around with the apes. It's not entirely because the apes can be strong, tough, treacherous, and capable of delivering a nasty bite. Though these considerations are significant, the main obstacle is money. Apes are expensive to buy and maintain, whereas white rats can be purchased cheaply, demand very little in the way of care, and can be easily disposed of. Even cheaper for the experimenter is the college sophomore.

The apes got a chance to show their stuff through a happenstance. Just before World War I the Germans established a station in the Canary Islands for the study of anthropoids. Köhler, a Gestalt psychologist, was sent to the station to study chimps. When the war broke out, Köhler was trapped at the station and therefore had plenty of time to carry on his studies. He suspected that Thorndike's procedures and interpretations were incorrect. He felt that the apes would display insight if given the chance. A chance involved allowing the animal to see the elements of the situation that confronted him.

Of course, to show learning via insight there had to be a suitable problem. The first approach was to place a banana out of direct reach and leave the chimp to get it with the materials at his disposal. If a banana outside of the cage were tied to a string that did reach the cage, the chimp would haul in the banana right away. The chimps learned to use sticks also to pull in bananas. One chimp even figured out how to join two pieces of bamboo together to reach a banana that was too far away for either stick. If a banana were placed too high to be reached directly, the apes easily learned to move a box under the food. Some of them learned to place one box on top of another, though such structures tended to be unstable. Engineers they were not. But they surely showed insight. We have to remember that in the coaching situation.

Figuring Out Personality

With the inevitable growth of sports psychology we will be increasingly confronted by the term "personality," along with its accompanying theories and tests. Already, personality tests form the vanguard of sports psychology. More and more we are going to hear about the relationship between personality and athletic achievement. Sports psychology is going to lean heavily for its research, explanations, and guides to action on personality theories and personality tests.

Those interested in the psychology of sports will want to put themselves in the best possible positions to evaluate and make use of the results, views, and suggestions offered by professional psychologists and other scientists. Interest in personality has always existed, with a consequent enormous literature, a literature that continues to grow. Most of the publications concerned with personality can be classified under one of several headings, such as the literary, the theoretical, and the quantitative. Since the literature is bulky enough to defy complete coverage, even by the professional, it's useful to have some kind of road map, even if crude, to afford us some orientation.

Attempts to define / When we were young, most of us thought of personality as a given quantity or thing that made one sought after or influential. In high school the classmate with "personality" was elected to class offices, had many friends, was always going out on dates. I suppose that most of us viewed personality as a mysterious kind of thing but a reality that produced results. Whatever it was, we just wished that we had more of it. Such a perception is still prevalent even among adults. An individual is often mentioned as having "loads of personality," while someone else is thought to have "no personality." Many world leaders have come into power, by election or otherwise, because of their "personality." To most professionals such a concept of personality seems naive and useless. However, the common view may prove to be not all that bad. From the scientific viewpoint, an individual's impact on others may turn out to be a critical aspect of his personality. But, the difficulty for researching is that personality, as used in the popular sense, represents the impact of a package made up of ingredients in complex combinations. For example, some of the important ingredients would likely be wit, intelligence, social perception, extroversion, courage, apparent honesty, voice, appearance. Research efforts become extremely difficult when the researcher must deal with a conglomeration of traits.

Many definitions of personality have been put forth by eminent psychologists, and all of these definitions have been criticized. The criticisms tend to fall into one of two classes: the definition is too inclusive; the definition is not inclusive enough. Apparently, delicate phrasing is needed to strike the right balance. There are two groups of critics who object to all definitions of personality. One group takes the position that since each personality is unique, the topic is not susceptible to scientific treatment. Hence, why bother with definitions? They proclaim a kind of futility. They point out that, like snowflakes, no two personalities are exactly alike, though there is surely no way of verifying such a statement. It surely has to be conceded that snowflakes vary greatly in their designs. But that's not the slightest reason to avoid studying the formation of a snowflake. The other group of critics seems to think that we should not define personality simply because we're not yet ready for definitions. Their position is that we should defer definitions until they almost emerge by themselves. That is, the findings will compel the best of definitions. Such a view doesn't seem too bad.

Regardless of the definitions of personality that guide our thinking and research, we have to realize that no matter how clearly we seem to understand a personality trait in a person whom we know, the trait is never *directly* perceived. Our perception is always based on inferences we draw from observed behavior (which is also indirectly perceived). You can describe almost anyone whom you know well on the bases of his traits. But you've made up your mind about his traits by watching his behavior. If he's always avoided paying his share of the dinner bill, you know him to be penurious, which is just another word for tightwad. If he is generally in good humor and likes to laugh, you think of him as jolly. In such a mental process you've generalized from behavior or abstracted a trait. Generalizations and abstractions are a necessary part of the adjustment process for all of us. We have to assign traits to people in order to make sense of them. But this approach, which we, as laymen, need, holds difficulties for the scientific study of personality. Not only are traits abstractions, but these abstractions have to be compounded to form additional and weaker abstractions. It's easy for our chain of thinking to acquire links of sand.

Early history / For good and sufficient reasons we usually trace most intellectual efforts back to that remarkable community, the ancient Greeks of Athens. Theophrastus, throughout his long life, was intensively interested in character structure, but he didn't feel qualified to write about his observations until he was ninety-nine years old. He apparently wanted to wait and be sure he had a good look at things before committing himself. He claimed his great longevity as his main qualification to offer comment. Theophrastus's book is still read for its insights into character as well as for its style. He was most perplexed and fascinated by the fact that the Greeks, who seemed homogeneous in culture, traditions, and education, and who all lived in the same climate, could produce such diverse character structures.

It seems almost certain that there was a normal distribution of traits among the Greeks. However, Theophrastus fastened on instances of extreme traits and then built personality portraits around such extremes. Some modern psychologists might object to such a procedure, but there may be something pertinent to high-level sports performance in the portraits of Theophrastus. It seems possible that for some great athletic performers a single aspect of personality can be so extreme and dominant as to push nearly every other trait into the background.

Throughout the ages character portrayal has been the most essential aspect of literature. Even the most ingenious plot would be dull if the reader does not understand the main characters. The great novelists and playwrights have brilliantly displayed character by way of both descriptions and glimpses of key behavior. They leave us astounded by their penetrating insights into personality. In the great works of literature the chief characters have personalities that are not only consistent with behavior, but their personalities actually determine their behavior. Hamlet's character is clearly depicted, and he acts in accordance with his character. Shakespeare's play would have no impact if Hamlet, uncharacteristically, had eloped with Ophelia. Dickens's characters were most vividly portrayed and for the most part consistent in behavior. But Dickens was an optimist who believed that a highly charged emotional experience could change character for the better (an idea that is beginning to intrigue psychotherapists). The corrective emotional experience appears often in the works of Dickens. The most familiar example is that of Scrooge, who changed from a hardhearted person into rather a pleasant chap. But then any of us could be shaken up by visits from several ghosts.

The early experimental psychologists were not at all interested in personality as a formal subject. In their searching for universals personality differences were a nuisance to them. Not so with the analysts, who considered personality to be central to behavior and health. The personality theories of Freud, along with their later modifications, are more than ever with us. Jung's terms "introvert–extrovert" are still household words. Those psychiatrists who were not within the analytic fold seemed to deal in symptoms rather than theories. But it was this interest in the symptoms of mental disturbance that helped to supply the items for the first large-scale personality testing—Woodworth's "Personal Data Sheet," which was administered to soldiers during World War I. A proliferation of personality tests followed.

Traits / The notion of traits is a literary one. Nevertheless, it looks as if behavioral scientists will of necessity be dealing with traits for a long time to come. The scientists must be feeling a sense of uneasiness. The task for them would seem to be to make our concepts of traits and the names assigned to them as realistic as possible. As suggested, traits are abstractions and derive from a literary heritage. Two psychologists once took the trouble to count some 18,000 trait names, most of them from literature. This remarkable number could immediately be reduced somewhat because many trait names were synonymous. Still, a lot of the terms remain, and psychologists have been trying to boil them down to manageable proportions. This job presents all manner of complications. At times, it seemed that many traits correlated highly enough to be lumped together into a master trait. But at other times what appeared to be a single trait was found to contain a number of traits. Even many years ago, the studies of Hartshorne and May showed that such an apparently simple trait as honesty in children is far from simple. For example, it was discovered that some children would lie but not cheat on an exam—and vice versa. Hugh Hartshorne and Mark May reached the conclusion that there is no general trait of honesty or dishonesty. As another example, Jung's notion of introversion–extroversion looked fairly straightforward and solid, but exploration by a top statistician revealed that it comprised many other traits.

An interesting and significant statistical method that has been used by psychologists is factor analysis. Put briefly, the method was designed to uncover dimensions. As used in personality testing, factor analysis was intended to reveal a clustering of trait items and in this way reduce the number of trait names. Many clusterings have been reported, but the Copernican promise has not been fulfilled.

All in all, our efforts to understand behavior seem destined to live with the notion of traits for a long time. We will remain hopeful that along the way psychologists will improve their ideas of traits and develop instruments that will measure them better.

Personality types / I think that many of us embrace the idea of types, probably because this simple delusion gives us a feeling of comfort and security. If, in dealing with another person, we feel we know "his type," we can then predict his behavior and perhaps take the action that seems best for us. If there were clear and valid types of personality it would surely simplify our task of adjusting to others. How easily perceptions and actions would follow. But as much as the notion of personality types has been entertained by the general public, this idea does not get much support from science.

One of the most familiar sights for the psychology student is the display of the bell-shaped, or normal, distribution curve. It is pointed out to the student that practically everything that is measured about human beings tends to produce such a curve of distribution. The measurements include not only those of personality but also those of just about anything else. For example, if we measure the heights of a large group of people, the heights will be distributed in a bell-shaped curve, with most people being not far from the center. Obviously, when we move toward one extreme of the curve, the people become taller and taller, and, as we go back across the curve to the other extreme, the people become shorter. If we consider the entire curve, we see that the continuum is smooth. There are no breaks or irregularities that would suggest types. So we have to feel uneasy and arbitrary if we try to classify all people as "tall types," "short types," or "average types." In most cases a typing would mean nothing. It would only be meaningful for a few. And if we can assume, as we presumably should, that all or nearly all traits are distributed in a similar manner, then the search for personality traits has limited usefulness.

To summarize briefly, most measurements we can take of human beings tend to distribute themselves normally, and for this reason we cannot type the great majority of people. I think the practice of typing can be useful if we don't try to apply it to all people—that is, we should not try to force all people into Procrustean beds. Where typing can be usefully employed, it should be. Returning to our simple example of height, it seems likely that the only people whose life-styles are going to be highly affected by their heights are those who are at the extremes of a distribution. If a person is eight feet tall we can't simply dismiss him by giving him a standard score, as we could to anybody in the middle of the distribution. His great height is likely to dominate his life. The same holds true for the person who is four feet tall. Now, suppose we could measure a trait such as aggressiveness reasonably well. Almost certainly it, like height, is normally distributed. To push along further, it does not seem unreasonable to think that a person's aggressiveness is significant only when it is at an extreme. We might find someone who is so aggressive that in a statistical sense he is comparable to the person who is eight feet tall. Aggressiveness could—in an athlete, or someone else—be such a powerful "trait" that it dominates behavior. The label of "aggressive type" could be useful in some cases.

Reliability of tests / The concept of reliability applies to all measuring instruments no matter what they are measuring. In a field like physics the instruments are so superbly reliable that the only weak spot is the human reader. The instruments of psychology are not nearly that good.

The reliabilities of performance measurement in most sports are rather high. For example, in the shot put, the shot upon landing leaves a hole in the ground or a mark of some kind. If we give steel tapes to ten people and ask each individually to measure the distance of a given put, they will probably all agree to within half an inch. Such a measurement process has high reliability. The same reliability would be shown by a group of experienced timers holding stopwatches on a running or swimming race. They would be highly reliable in the sense that there would be substantial agreement among them. Each individual measurement would represent a result involving a mechanical instrument and the person operating it. Of course, the agreement or reliability would be even greater if the measurements of separate electronic timing devices were compared with each other. The "human factor" would be reduced.

In mental or personality measurment there is usually a "score," for the most part numerical. But the score is not objective. Though the tester may use some sort of instrument, supposedly objective, the tester's personality becomes involved and surely influences scores. Probably the most unreliable instrument for personality testing is the psychiatric interview. The psychiatrist becomes the instrument, and even if his insights are brilliant the process is not scientific. The Rorschach test lies in a kind of middle area. In this test of personality the blots do exist. There are ten cards and there are standard procedures for administering the test. But the tester greatly influences scoring by both the climate that he creates during testing and by the ways he handles the responses of the subject. In group tests the instrument has to stand more on its own with a greater hope of increased reliability. For example, if I were to administer a group intelligence or personality test, my influence should presumably be minimal.

Reliability is best served by testing instruments that produce consistent results. It's obviously better to measure distances with a steel tape than a rubber one. If testers used rubber tape measures, there would not be much agreement among them. In checking on reliability, *agreement* is the key word. It's possible to have reliability without an understanding of the process by which judgment is made. Not likely but possible. For example, if different psychiatrists independently assess the same subjects and agree on their findings, even though their processes were nonscientific, we have to concede reliability. We haven't had to do so thus far.

Most psychological tests have been constructed in such a way as to demonstrate their reliabilities. The agreement of a test lies within itself. If a number of test items are supposed to measure a certain factor, then the items can be divided into two groups and produce two scores. The agreement between the two scores is considered an index of reliability. Another way of estimating reliability of a test is to use the instrument a second time or more with the same subjects. The amount of agreement between the first and second scores seems to provide an estimate of the test's reliability. This method seems all right, but it could be misleading if what's being measured happens to change during the interval between tests. For example, a bathroom scale is almost completely reliable. You can weigh people and have great confidence in the reliability of the scale. But if you were to weigh the same people after an interval, you might record different weights for each. Some of the subjects may have been dieting and others overeating. The scale, as a measuring instrument, could be badly underestimated.

The product–moment correlation is the common statistical method used to express a test's reliability. Theoretically, correlations can vary all the way from 0.00 (no demonstrated relationship) to plus or minus 1.00 (perfect relationship, like the relationship between the diameter of a circle and its radius). Perfect relationships have never been seen in the world of behavior measurements, nor ever will be. For any personality test a reliability in the area of .90 would be highly acceptable, though we usually have to settle for much lower reliabilities. In testing for reliabilities, the size of a product–moment correlation will be affected by an artifact, the homogeneity of the population involved. If the spread in scores (standard deviation) of the subjects is large, the correlation turns out to be larger and vice versa.

Validity / The second important statistical aspect of a test, validity, is, like reliability, usually expressed by a statistical correlation. But the problem of estimating test validity is much more difficult than estimating reliability. The validity of a test indicates the extent to which it measures what it purports to measure. Traditionally, the validity of a test is measured against outside criteria. There's the rub! Satisfactory criteria for measuring a personality trait really don't exist. If such outside criteria were available there would be no need for a new test unless it could measure the trait more conventiently and inexpensively. In general, the "outside criteria" have low reliabilities, a fact which dooms a new test measured against them to a low validity. For example, a new test designed to measure a trait will produce scores that may then be correlated with the ratings of experts. But if the ratings of the experts are not in substantial agreement with each other, there is no mathematical chance for the new test to exhibit statistical validity.

Since the quantitative demonstration of validity is so difficult, as a practical matter, the amount of use that a personality test gets usually depends on its prestige and the feelings of the testers. Perhaps partly as a result of the prestige of a test and partly as a result of his own experience, the tester develops confidence in certain tests.

The task of validating a prediction is rather different from that of validating the measurement of a trait. If, for example, the object of a test is to predict who will drop out of school, who will be institutionalized for mental illness, or who will do well in athletics, validation of the test is a relatively simple matter. The test is first administered to an appropriate group; then a waiting period ensues in order to see what happens. If a test turns out to have predictive value, then it becomes a useful empirical instrument. Such a successful instrument surely would be welcome enough, but it would not in itself advance our theoretical understanding of personality.

SOME TEST METHODS

Athletic coaches and physical educators who are interested in sports psychology will find themselves confronted by an increasingly expanding labyrinth of possible personality testing methods. Each of us has to work out his own orientation. Though the maze looks a bit complicated, a frame of reference can be helpful along the way. We have to make some response to the commercial instruments that already are being offered.

Rating scales / The process in which one person evaluates another has always been with us. The letter of recommendation, though regarded with skepticism, is still prevalent. The basic wisdom may be that there's something wrong with a chap who hasn't got a few friends who are willing to perjure themselves in his behalf. The rating scale emerged as a method of systematizing the observations and inferences that one person makes concerning another. The basic idea seems good, but it has certain difficulties. Among the difficulties are the fact that the rater has prejudices either for or against the subject and that there are differences in observational opportunities. In a real sense the rater becomes the "instrument." If we ask the rater to report only on behavior that he thinks he has observed, we are asking him to be a kind of reporting instrument. But, as is more commonly the case, if we ask the rater to make an assessment of a personality trait, we are putting the "instrument" to a task that is more than reportorial.

One of the most significant things about us, as people, is that we present different facets of ourselves to different people. Suppose the personality of an athlete is being investigated, and one of the items to be rated is, "Does he talk much?" Further, suppose the raters are his coach, his roommates, and his girlfriend. The coach may check "never talks," the roommates "about average," and his girlfriend "talks all the time." Results like these might seem inconsistent and discouraging to the tester, who is looking for close agreement among raters. But such diverse ratings might represent important psychological information about the subject. We get estimates of his behavior that take account of context. For example, if we accept the coach as a good observer, which he is likely to be, then we have the significant information that the athlete "never talks" *in the presence of his coach.*

The published statistical reliabilities of ratings are erratic and generally low. Validities of rating scales are hard to measure because often outside criteria do not exist for a particular item being rated. In rating scales, reliability and validity become intertwined. Some psychologists have even taken the position that reliability and validity are the same—i.e., if enough people agree that you've got a certain trait, you've got it.

Many psychologists, after looking at the published findings, are discouraged with rating scales as useful instruments. There surely are difficulties, but much of the use of ratings has been incredibly naive. With more realistic and sophisticated development the scales should become a highly valuable class of instruments. They should have special value in sports psychology, where observational opportunities are so good.

Paper and pencil tests / The questionnaire is probably the most widely used instrument for personality diagnosis. With the blooming of sports psychology, athletes, coaches, and others connected with sports can expect an increasing flood of inventories and other questionnaires.

As mentioned earlier, Woodworth's "Personal Data Sheet" seems to have started the whole movement. Confronted by millions of recruits, the Army was interested in predicting who would be likely to crack up in combat. Woodworth's questionnaire amounted to a list of items that experts felt were indicative of poor mental health. In the time since Woodworth, a great many questionnaires have been devised, many of them having a kind of psychiatric flavor. The underlying idea of personality inventories is about as follows: if the person who fills out the questionnaire professes or confesses to having the symptoms associated with those of mental patients, the subject is likely to be emotionally disturbed. Actually, the inventories have never worked out too well and have not become effective diagnostic instruments. Part of the trouble may be that the questionnaires are administered under a variety of psychological climates. The person who is seeking psychiatric help is bound to answer differently from the person who is seeking a job. There surely is a need to set up different norms for different situations.

The later questionnaires or inventories seem to represent a mixture of efforts to measure theoretically specified traits and to provide empirical keys for various categories. In general, the newer questionnaires appear to be more sophisticated than earlier ones in that they attempt to build in checks and balances. For example, there are items designed to indicate a subject's tendency to lie or mislead. Yet we don't know how good these checks and balances are.

The questionnaire certainly holds a fascination for most of us. Many self-administered personality tests in the form of questionnaires appear in newspapers and magazines. Of course, these questionnaires tend to be grossly unscientific, but their popularity does indicate widespread interest and even belief in them. It probably has to be conceded that the questionnaire method hasn't yet turned out to be all it was cracked up to be. But still, this method is not going to be discarded. We are already working with it in sports psychology.

Projective tests / The introduction of projective testing techniques into psychology has surely been one of the most imaginative steps taken in the study of personality. Man has always "seen things" in shadows or shapes in the night or clouds drifting overhead. For example, a cloud, or a part of it, may commonly be perceived as a human head, an animal, or almost anything. This kind of perception is different, at least in degree, from the perceptions we make in carrying out our everyday affairs. In the ordinary instances of a chair, a table, a book, the stimulus situation is compelling enough to make nearly all of us come up with about the same labels. However, if we are confronted by more ambiguous stimuli, our "inner processes" play a much greater role in determining the perceptions. There is room for individual expression, and, hopefully, significant aspects of the personality will be revealed.

In the presentation of a stimulus situation for possible projection there has to be a critical point between definite structure and no structure at all. Clearly structured material would elicit an easy flow of responses but little or no projection. Completely unstructured material would lack stimulus value, and there would be few or no responses.

The Rorschach test, introduced in 1921, remains the most famous of all the projective testing devices. The test materials consist of ten cards. Each card has an "ink blot" that is symmetrical and intricate. Some cards are entirely in black and gray; some contain a splash of color along with black and gray, while others are all or nearly all in color. The tester presents the cards to the subject one at a time and in a prescribed order. Responses and other observations are recorded by the tester. There is a second pass through the cards during which the tester makes "inquiries." There are scores and interpretations of scores. All in all, the process is complicated, and the tester has to be specially trained.

Rorschach believed that specific scores would be directly diagnostic of personality. Had it worked out that way, his test would have been universally accepted as a vital scientific instrument. But the direct scores didn't show much, and the scoring of the Rorschach test has become incredibly complex and almost cultist. The extreme Rorschachers have an almost religious belief in and fervor about their work. They do not welcome statistical investigations of the reliability and validity of their methods.

It's hard to believe that ten little ink blots have led to such a vast literature, the widespread use of a clinical testing method, and so much controversy and emotion. I remember being in a graduate class in which an eminent professor wanted to make a distinction between scientific and nonscientific psychology. He seized on the Rorschach test as an example of nonscientific psychology. In my opinion he was right, but for weeks the room was in an uproar. Every other concept that the professor had intended to teach was driven aside by some students' heated defenses of the ink blot test. The besieged professor had only wanted to make a passing reference to the Rorschach to illustrate a point, but unfortunately for him there happened to be several devout Rorschachers in the room. The emotional claims made for the Rorschach test ran almost to the diagnosis of an ingrown toenail.

We seem to have a draw between the formal psychologists and the Rorschachers, a draw that may never be played off. Most psychometricians have all but dismissed the Rorschach test as unscientific in that it has no solid norms, depends on the intuitions of the testers, and has no experimental verification. For the most part the Rorschach test has an attraction but little scientific standing. The Rorschachers seem to have a fervent belief in their instrument and will continue to use it regardless of the challenges or charges brought against it.

The Thematic Apperception Test (TAT) / Developed by Henry Murray, this projection test may be as widely used as the Rorschach. The TAT employs a rather different type of projection than the Rorschach. Pictures are shown to a subject, and he is asked to create a story about each one. In contrast to the blots of the Rorschach, the stimuli of the TAT are not very ambiguous. For example, the ages and sex of the characters in the pictures are for the most part readily identifiable. Also, their facial expressions provide clues. Apparently, the rationale is that some of the characters in the pictures can be perceived as important figures in the subject's life story. The ways in which the subject weaves these figures into narratives can reveal his attitudes toward key figures, especially family members, who have been instrumental in the formation of his personality. Further, the themes may suggest to the subject his needs and fantasies.

It seems likely that anyone who writes a story expresses something of his or her personality, but the directness of expression must vary with age and sophistication. The child expresses his needs without much inhibition. High school and college youngsters probably have more defenses. As a person's sophistication grows, it becomes difficult to know to what extent a story is expressive of his personality. A great novelist, for example, is so good at his trade that he can depict many diverse characters, some of them no doubt with certain aspects of his own character, but others totally invented.

Efforts to make statistical evaluations of the reliability and validity of the TAT have encountered difficulties even greater than those met in assessing the Rorschach. For one thing, the scoring of the TAT is even looser. Those who would like to take a scientific approach to describing, measuring, or predicting human behavior would be delighted if the projective tests had been able to demonstrate objectivity and statistical evidence of reliability and validity. But so far it hasn't worked that way, and the tests remain in the artistic area rather than in the scientific.

What now? We can't really have reliable instruments for testing personality until we have better ideas of what it is that we are testing. Our theories about personality have to be sounder, more widely elaborated. Diverse hypotheses have to be unified. It may take an Einstein to do it. Meanwhile, we know that in sports psychology we are going to have to deal more and more with personality even though theory and testing are still in a primitive state.

The Coach

Any effort to understand sports psychology must involve the athletic coach. The coach has become a gigantic figure in the sports world. He is, in fact, so central to athletics that we must understand him before we can understand athletics. For the sports psychologist the coach will be both a vital subject and a valuable source of observations. In the following pages we will be looking at the phenomenal rise to stardom of the coach. His history supplies some useful perspective. Also, we will be talking about the coach's expertise, his task, his personality, and some of the difficulties he encounters.

The rise of the coach / In view of the American coach's present prestige and power, it may seem that it has always been that way. It hasn't. The coach's rise to power has been relatively recent. Even early in this century the college coach had little or no standing. College sports activities were entirely controlled by the athletes, who organized their own competitions. The first contests were intramural. Then the competition spread beyond the walls, the athletes in one university seeking competition with the athletes of other universities. All the arrangements were made by the athletes themselves. In those days there were no coaches, no athletic directors, and no formal recognition of the teams by university authorities. In England, where traditions live longer, university athletics remain similar to what they were in America some seventy years ago. Athletes in English universities have their own clubs, which are not officially related to the university, and make their own arrangements for training and competition. If there is a coach, he has been hired by the students. The coach exercises no direction but rather waits patiently in the background to be consulted.

. In the early part of this century the club system was the hub of athletics in the United States. Athletes formed clubs to foster their sports and to arrange competition with other clubs. The clubs flourished, but college athletics soon began to show signs of the enormous growth that was to come. In both the club and the college settings, coaching was informal, almost incidental. Coaches were mostly unpaid volunteers. At a university, the previous year's team captain might return to help out. But he had no real power. The clubs often relied for coaching help on members who were past their peaks and were no longer active competitors.

With the rapid rise of college sports the clubs began to decline. Athletes who in the past would have gotten jobs with a club and competed under its name now began to go to the universities on "athletic scholarships." The meeting places of most of the formerly prominent athletic clubs became luncheon spots for businessmen of certain ethnic groups. Though the real reason for the existence of the clubs had disappeared, some of them tried to keep athletics going on a limited basis. "Athletic memberships" were given to selected outstanding athletes with the tacit understanding that the athletes were not to exercise real membership privileges.

Many of the early American coaches started as workers in the athletic fields. Gradually they discarded their rakes and shovels and spent more time in the training rooms. From the training rooms they returned in time to the athletic fields, but this time without rakes and shovels. These precursors of modern coaching seemed to have had a number of characteristics in common. They had themselves done rather well in club athletics. They had very little formal education. They were shrewd. They wanted to make a living out of athletics. They became colorful figures and, apparently, effective coaches.

Among the early coaches training methods were closely guarded secrets. When the coach prescribed a workout, the athlete was not let in on the rationale behind it, probably because there wasn't any. In the training rooms they had mysterious and magical rubbing compounds that offered the athlete an edge over his competitors. Did the coach believe in his magical mixtures? Or was he more likely a kind of practical psychologist?

For some unknown reason the early American coaches had longevity enough to confuse any insurance actuarial table. Some continued to coach even into their eighties and nineties. They were still around when I was a young coach, but every time one dropped by the wayside, he was replaced by a university graduate. The old fraternity grew smaller and then finally faded away.

In the early days the social position of the coach was low, and so was his pay. He was someone to listen to on the athletic field but not a person to invite to dinner. His social status was somewhat similar to that of a gardener or a janitor. As a matter of fact, as recently as a generation ago some of the English coaches were responsible for cleaning up and weeding. Among many British sportsmen the professional coach is still regarded as a kind of intruder, a sort of evil and perhaps not even a necessary one.

Today, in the United States the athletic coach usually enjoys great prestige in his community. Some football coaches could be elected to high political office in their states if they wanted to go that route. The dramatic rise in the prestige of the coach surely has its sociological complexities, but the outline of the story would seem to be as follows. At one time in the northeastern part of the United States, the universities were somewhat attuned to the British view of athletics. Not only that, the society of the area remained much more stratified than it did in the rest of the nation. But there came the rapid growth of educational institutions throughout the South, the Midwest, the Southeast, and the West Coast. Small colleges, especially the state ones, became gigantic universities. These new university giants had only remote connections with European traditions and practices. And most of the people living in the areas of these new universities had relatively little sense of social class. Thus, the setting was ideal for the rise of the new class of professional athletic coaches. In terms of athletic performance the rest of the world has been closing in on the United States, and the reason is primarily that in most countries an honored class of professional coaches has been emerging. A formerly downtrodden group is at last getting respect and greater monetary rewards.

The coach and the administration / Many university administrators, especially in the Northeast, are uneasy about the athletic picture getting too big. They are concerned that what they think of as the sideshow of sports will distract students and faculty from the main arena of classroom teaching. They feel that there is a threat to the teaching hierarchy. The typical Ivy League administrator, for example, would like a sports program that seems to serve the nebulous needs of the students but is not prominent enough to cast a shadow over the school's academic reputation. He doesn't want the athletic teams to be badly beaten in intercollegiate athletics, but neither does he wish to see the teams become powerhouses. A 50–50 win–loss record is about right. This position, when taken by the administration, can produce a frustrated and puzzled coach. The more effectively he coaches, the more he will be cut down by the admissions office: fewer good athletes will be admitted.

In sharp contrast to the conservative private universities, many of the large state universities permit a coach to recruit almost any high school athlete whom he wants, the numbers of such athletes being limited only by a budget. Incredible as it may seem, athletes who could neither read nor write have been admitted to universities. But in return for such extraordinary freedom in recruiting, the coach *must* produce winning teams. In the Ivy League schools and in similar institutions, where the administrators are aware that the coach is restricted in his selection of future players, some sort of sheltering blanket is offered to the coach, although the blanket has a few holes in it. The popular coach can survive a few bad seasons—but not many. If the Ivy League coach feels bottled up by recruiting restrictions and decides to move along to a big-time athletic school, he should know that all shelter is gone. He has to produce winners.

The coach and the alumni / Some years ago the topic of the coach and the alumni would have required considerable space. These days, the account can be brief. The great power once exerted by the alumni has diminished. At one time, they could fire the coach and the athletic director. They could also threaten the security of the university president's job. They demanded to be heard, and they were heard. But now, the aging alumnus, with his raccoon coat, banner, and bottle, is largely a subject for the comic strip artists.

A generation or so ago, graduates used to come back to their colleges to "show the boys how to do it." Their purposes and activities were touching but unrealistic. Coaching had become complicated and intense. There was no longer a place for well-meaning amateurs. Teams had to be coached by professionals. When that realization took hold in most of the alumni, they turned their efforts toward criticizing the coaches and trying to switch the professionals at the helm.

Even as the alumni position weakens and becomes a bit comical, especially in the eyes of the undergraduates, it would be foolish for either the university administrators or the coaches to try to shut them out of the picture. The most obvious contribution of the alumni is financial. Some private universities are now in the process of raising more than $100 million, money that has to come from the alumni. Even from the standpoint of the coach there are contributions—other than the obvious financial ones— that the alumni can make. For example, the athletes like to know that there has been continuity of tradition in their sport and present interest from those who have gone before. Knowing that the sport has deep roots in the university, the athlete is motivated to excel. For the most part the alumni want only to participate—they want to be "helpful"; they want to contribute ideas, even though they haven't the slightest notion of how naive their ideas may be to the professional coach. But the astute coach remains calm and fields the suggestions with ease. One top football coach showed me a play that he'd received from an alumnus. The basic difficulty with the play was that it took fourteen men to execute it. The coach wrote a letter of appreciation.

The technical competence of the coach / It's difficult to generalize about the expertise of the athletic coach. The range of individual abilities seems very great. There are surely coaches who are highly expert in their sports, and there are those who are incompetent. No doubt the same situation exists in other professions, such as law or medicine. The most accurate evaluations of a coach's technical competence could probably be made by his close colleagues, but they are not likely to express their feelings publicly. Another source of assessment would be the athletes themselves, but this source is tricky in that it can reflect personality factors.

Technical competence may be highest among football coaches, with perhaps basketball running a close second. The football coach puts in long hours and expends enormous effort battling for his survival. Football pays the freight for the other sports. Pressure is great. There is very little room for an incompetent football coach.

The track and field coach may, in some respects, have the most difficult situation of all. He is responsible for the teaching of many skills, and it is just about impossible for him to be expert in all of them. To add to his difficulties, what he has to learn about the many events he coaches must be learned very early in his coaching career. Only the young coach can appear ignorant by asking naive questions. Later on, when perhaps the coach is considered a sage, the same questions cannot be asked because they would shock both the athletes and the other coaches. The young track coach should almost "run scared" to fortify himself with a knowledge of fundamentals and face-to-face coaching experience in as many events as possible. But he usually doesn't. He doesn't labor under the same pressure that plagues the football coach. Because track and field does not bring in money, losing seasons can be tolerated. A track coach is seldom fired, especially if he has a pleasing personality. During his tenure, he may make many friends and political allies, which will result in his being appointed to the coaching staffs of international teams. Some kind of uniform usually goes along with the appointment. For example, a member of the Olympic staff gets a cap with appropriate insignia. Upon returning home he may wear it to practice in the pathetic hope that the members of his team will be persuaded to carry out his instructions because of the prestige suggested by his little cap.

Psychologists who are interested in sports behavior have a tendency to turn toward track and field for their material. This is natural enough because there are many events in track and field, and all of them are quantitative. However, in exploring the behavior of a track-and-field athlete or, for that matter, any athlete, particularly his response to the coaching situation, the psychologist can go badly astray if he assumes professional competency even on the part of a nationally prominent coach.

Coaching personality / The basic task of the coach is to modify behavior. Behavior modification is also the main task of most other professionals such as salesmen, politicians, teachers, psychiatrists, military leaders, and revolutionaries. The task of each of these groups seems clear in outline. The salesman confronts someone who appears unwilling to buy. The task is to influence that person to buy. The politician wants his subject to vote in a certain way. The psychiatrist would like his patient to change his behavior in a manner that would bring the patient less personal misery and make him more effective in dealing with life. And so it goes. From observation we can be sure that a diversity of personalities can operate to produce behavior changes in others. However, there is surely a relationship between personality and the situation in which change is sought. For example, a salesman may be highly effective in dealing with certain products and people but ineffective in other situations. A psychiatrist may be superb with some patients but not with others.

In dealing with the coach's ability to modify behavior, it's useful, I think, to consider personality types. The notion of personality types has to be presented with great hesitancy and a recognition of the scientific difficulties involved. Types tend to be oversimplifications, and they usually can include only extreme cases. Most psychologists have discarded the use of types. Still, anyone who has been close to the coaching picture might find the following dichotomy to be useful and realistic.

Among the coaching personalities there is Coach A, the colorful, flamboyant, aggressive coach. He tends to argue with officials and have temper tantrums in public. You've seen some of them on national television. Then there is Coach B, who operates somewhat in the manner of a nondirective psychotherapist. He makes no effort to be a colorful leader. His temperament probably wouldn't allow it anyway. Instead, he represents a kind of resource to the athletes—a resource that's available to aid them in working out certain problems, either technical or personal. He is given more to calm dialogue and careful listening than to speechmaking. Through his approach and personality he is often effective in bringing about important and deep-seated changes in behavior. Changes in attitude and performance are related. Both types of coaching personalities are apparently needed. Each can have a critical function. Coach A is at his best in a leadership position in which group attitudes are to be influenced. In a minor way the A coach can be compared to some of the great leaders in history, many of whom, though shrewd, were egocentric and emotionally immature. In contrast, Coach B is most effective on a one-to-one basis. He can have a profound influence on individual athletes but less influence on group behavior.

Both A and B operate well in their appropriate spheres while in other areas their effectiveness declines. A very few coaches seem talented and flexible enough to operate as either A or B, but such an extraordinary ability to adjust is not really prevalent. In general, the coach's personality ought to be appropriate to his specific coaching situation. For example, in football the colorful leader tends to be the head coach and B an assistant. It may well be that B is the better technician and teacher, but it also may be that he is destined to remain an assistant coach.

Like the rest of us, the coach is strongly affected by his feelings of personal security. And, of course, these feelings are tied to an entire biography and personality structure. An important part of biography for the coach is his own record as an athlete. The ex–all-American and the former Olympic champ seldom become great coaches. Most successful coaches have had mediocre personal athletic records. This pattern is truly curious because it usually takes a fine athletic record to get started in coaching. Yet there have been

Olympic track coaches who never made their own college teams. There was a famous Olympic swimming coach who couldn't swim.

Early in his coaching career the great college performer has a big edge over the mediocre performer or nonperformer. First, of course, the ex-great is much more likely to find a coaching job. In addition to whatever technical competence he may have he has a feel for what things are like in high-pressure competition. Also, his prestige is influential with those he coaches. The nonperformer starts his coaching career with a disadvantage. It takes him a while to catch up, but after that the advantage tends to be his.

The great performer has had his personal athletic achievement. There remains no large neurotic gap in the athletic career that needs closing. As the years pass by, the great performer's coaching duties tend to bore him. The "ho hum, another season" attitude is disastrous. Such an attitude is communicated to the youngsters on the squad. They become less enthusiastic, and the coach becomes less effective. In contrast, the advantage of the coach who was a nonperformer increases. His past failure to achieve outstanding personal performance has left a neurotic gap that will never be closed. His enthusiasm is maintained. He approaches each new season with a freshness that's contagious.

For most coaches there has to be a certain amount of personal insecurity. It's best if a nice balance can be struck. The completely secure coach won't have enough irritation, and for that reason he is not likely to keep running hard enough. The very insecure coach might run too much and too wildly, with injurious effects to his mental and physical health. Somewhere in between lies the happy medium.

Confusion / The average coach is an extremely well-adjusted person who tends to be in realistic contact with the environment. He is seldom a candidate for a mental institution. But there seems to be a tendency for the otherwise alert coach to fall into a confusion that can harm his athletes' performance and be injurious to his coaching career.

The dedicated coach gives time, energy, and concentration to his sport. His great devotion to coaching may involve nearly all of his waking moments—and his sleeping ones, too—in unconscious mental activity. Surely his intensity and absorption merit congratulations when there is an important team victory. (A typical television shot is that of the winning coach being congratulated by the losing coach.) The exhausted football coach has in his own way run with the ball carriers, blocked with the blockers, and passed with the quarterback. In a similar way the track coach throws with the throwers, jumps with the jumpers, sprints with the sprinters, and shares the fatigue of the distance runners. But a significant note of stark reality intercedes. The running, blocking, tackling, jumping, and throwing are carried out only by the athletes. The coach does none of it—not one single bit! The coach is not to be criticized for the empathy that creates the illusion that he has actually participated. But it is important for him to distinguish between illusion and reality. The inability to make such a distinction has wrecked many coaching careers.

The confusion may appear mild enough, but it tends to produce dangerous psychological results. The coach can fall into the view that the athletes are simply units to be used in his grand scheme—pawns to be maneuvered on his chessboard. His main interest, which should be the athletes themselves, slips to the point where it is concerned only with the athletes' ability to carry out coaching designs. It's easy for the coach to get caught in such a trap. After all, the athletes come and go. The team and the institution go on forever—and the optimistic coach may think that he does too.

It seems unnecessary to say so, but the athlete is a living personality in dynamic interaction with his environment. He has hopes, dreams, frustrations, fears, successes, and defeats. It is foolish to regard him merely as a unit on a team. An athlete who feels that the coach perceives him as a pawn is bound to show diminished effort and enthusiasm. There will be resentment, even if not articulated, toward the coach who appears to exploit the athlete. A talented team can fall apart under this type of coaching.

Many coaches who had outstanding technical proficiency have gone down the drain because they failed to show interest in the individual personalities who made up their teams. One famous, well-publicized football coach at a great university became so confused that he thought the athlete should regard it as a great honor and privilege to become a unit under his masterly direction. The athletes felt otherwise. Their resentment grew to the point that they decided not to play at all if the coach remained. They meant it. For the first time in some eighty years this university, with its rich football tradition, would likely not have a team. The players presented the coach with an ultimatum—you leave or no team! The coach was thunderstruck by the ingratitude of the wretched players. But he did resign immediately. He may have remembered a saying that he used to quote in happier days: "If you are going to be thrown out of town, move fast and you'll look like you are leading a parade."

You might think that the performances of the high-level professional athletes would be unaffected by the degree of interest the coach takes in them personally. After all, the pros are supposed to be hard-bitten people who simply play for the money. But it doesn't work out that way. The pro, even though he earns a great deal of money, does not want to play for a coach who fails to recognize him as an individual. The players are making their reactions increasingly clear through their public comments and other behavior.

It is surprising and puzzling that the downfall of a great coach can come from a pattern of behavior that seems obvious enough to be easily avoided. It's just that the pattern is not easily avoided. For many coaches the trap is as inevitable as the head cold. Once a person's interests center about self-aggrandizement, his ability to influence others declines. Dale Carnegie's lectures and books present the same theme over and over: You influence people's behavior by turning your attention to them. In the cases of some of the great leaders in history, the Carnegie approach may have been strictly a technique. But genuine or artificial, it has worked. And when the leader has departed from this pattern, he has gotten into trouble.

Sports deserve publicity and thrive on it. The successful coach will be publicized. He has to accept the propaganda and central stage as necessary parts of the system. But to the extent that he can, the wise coach will keep the spotlight on the players. While accepting the system, he will avoid the mistake of being taken in by it.

The Coach
and the Athlete

Nearly all of the more than 100,000 athletic coaches in the nation carry out face-to-face coaching. The very few who don't are the head coaches of football at large institutions. In this section our concern is with that vast majority of face-to-face coaches and the realities they meet.

Coaching and teaching / There are similarities between classroom teaching and coaching on the field. In both activities a great premium is placed on achieving a clear and interesting presentation of a body of knowledge. The significant difference is in the depth of the responses that each method brings about. Classroom teaching often results in mere surface effects. The student may simply acquire new verbal responses that are quickly lost. After he takes his examinations, the lines of poetry and the critical dates of history he memorized begin to fade away. In contrast to academic teaching, effective coaching changes motor habits, and the changes must be solidly established.

An example may help to show the significant difference between teaching and coaching. Let's suppose a knowledgeable coach is working with a discus thrower. The coach explains and hammers away at the important points of discus technique. After a sustained period of coaching, there may be no observable change in the athlete's way of throwing. He may appear no closer to learning discus form than when he started. Yet the chances are that he can give an excellent verbal account of the various points of discus technique. Were he to take a paper and pencil test on the discus throw, he would probably get a high mark. But he has not changed his deep-rooted motor patterns. And he may never.

It's well worth belaboring the major distinction between academic teaching and coaching. Coaching is a kind of showdown affair. Effective coaching has to bring about a real change in behavior. Adding a bit to the subject's verbal repertory doesn't do much good. An understanding of the coaching task is necessary if we are to grasp the coach–athlete relationship.

Though coaching is a form of teaching, it probably comes much closer to psychotherapy in its intensity and in the effects it is meant to produce. Coaching and psychotherapy have close parallels. To be effective, both have to bring about real changes in behavior and perceptions. For both there are vital face-to-face relationships. One of the critical similarities is the subject's resistance to change, which can be powerful. Sometimes it can't be budged. Probably nobody knows what this type of resistance is all about. It may even be protective in a biological sense. Resistance to change may in some ways contribute to a stability and continuity of the personality. Regardless of its roots, the resistance of the athlete to behavior change is one of the highly significant facts of coaching.

Resistance by the athlete constantly jolts the self-image of the coach. The coach would like to think of himself as the learned and revered mentor. His idea of a good relationship might be to have the athlete hang on his every word of wisdom. The athlete, grateful for the advice given him by the beloved and respected coach, moves quickly to carry out instructions. But that isn't the way things go. One way or another resistance is likely to pop up. Sometimes the strength of the resistance and the ways of showing it can amount even to a form of hostility. It is natural enough for the coach to become upset. But it is professional of the coach to recognize that it's all in the day's work. And if he realizes that there may be nothing pathological about the youngster, he has taken a good first step. Also, resistance is usually an impersonal matter and does not indicate a dislike of a particular coach. It's just a part of the coaching process. Though it's not easy, a professional coach tries to keep his calm.

Resistance to behavioral change can show up in a number of ways. It's useful to look at some of these forms.

Breakdown in communication / When addressing an athlete the coach can often get the feeling that he is talking to a brick wall. The athlete may stare blankly as if he'd been able to turn off his hearing. The look of complete incomprehension is familiar to all experienced coaches. Even the simplest ideas may not be grasped by the athlete. There are very few staggering intellectual concepts in sports. Points of form are seldom so complicated as to baffle a normal brain. Yet no matter how well and how often a coach explains a point, the athlete may show an utter lack of comprehension. Frustration can easily lead the coach to condemn the athlete as being dumb. Stupidity, however, has nothing to do with the pattern. What we have is a form of resistance that is common to the coach–athlete relationship.

You almost have to witness the process of communication breakdown to believe it. In my early coaching days I could not believe that there could be such a disruption of communication. I think of two fine athletes who gave me what I then regarded as a tough time. They didn't accomplish much during their freshman years but both later went on to break all kinds of records.

In case A I repeated a simple point of technique in various ways. I then asked, "Tom, do you understand it?"

"I've got it. I've got it!" he answered.

I went over the point again. "Are you sure you understand?"

"I've got it. I've got it!"

"What have you got, Tom?"

"I don't know. I'm sorry. I wasn't really listening." This was progress. At least he was becoming aware of the communications problem.

Case B was a shot-putter of enormous athletic potential and high intelligence. His chief technical fault was that upon crossing the circle he landed with his right leg straight and in this way cut off much of his potential power. In my coaching I concentrated on the needed correction, and every day in practice I emphasized the need to bend the leg. The concept was easy enough. Yet my persistence over many weeks and hundreds of repetitions produced no visible results. One day the athlete put the shot eight feet farther than he ever had before. He came to me and said that he had made an important discovery. The discovery was that it was essential to bend the right leg. He then said, "Coach, I wish you had told me about that." He was completely sincere. That was his recollection of things.

When these two athletes became upperclassmen and top performers, they were thoroughly cooperative, and communication between us was clear and simple. An interesting footnote: They once reprimanded the freshmen, who didn't seem to be listening to me. A little bit of biography can easily be forgotten.

Challenging the workout for the day / Disagreement with coaching instruction and planning is a common form of resistance by the athlete. However, in the team sports there is much less chance for this type of expression to appear. For example, a football team's daily practice is usually carried out with great precision. The activities are conducted by the watch and the whistle. A certain time-period calls for a specific activity, calisthenics, for example, or windsprints. On the field there is practically no chance for the player to engage the coach in dialogue concerning the schedule of the day. In fact, the player may not know which coach on the staff planned the schedule for a particular day. Also, the player is thwarted by group suggestion, since everybody else on the squad seems to be going about things. In general, the protest has to be confined to griping to teammates and dogging it.

Disagreement with the coach's prescribed workout is strongest in the individual sports, especially running. Here, a number of factors magnify the possibilities of attacking the coach through disagreement. First, modern training methods make possible an almost infinite variety of daily workouts. The coach has to plan from general outlines and can never be sure that the workout he selects is the best one. He can never have full confidence in what he prescribes. Second, there is sometimes a little-understood wisdom of the body that can suggest an effective workout for a particular athlete. The Russian coaches have come to believe that this playback from the body should not be ignored. But in this view the Russians are mainly considering the advanced and perhaps gifted athlete. It seems unlikely that the average runner will have many valid clues as to what his workout should be. Yet, if he claims to have them the coach can't be sure he doesn't. Third, the coach usually prescribes the day's workout verbally, thus opening the door to dialogue.

The "expert" / A certain type of track-and-field athlete pores over all the publications dealing with his event. He reads the journals and books with a view, conscious or unconscious, to giving the coach an uneasy time. He looks for material written by so-called authorities that will contradict the teachings of the coach. Such articles are not hard to find because, after all, the authorities contradict each other. In his reading the athlete also tries to discover points about which the coach may be ignorant. It is possible to make an assiduous search of the literature and come up with something the coach doesn't know much about. The coach doesn't have the time to read all articles on all events. The athlete who specialized in a single event has a jump on the busy coach, who must spread his energy and time thinly over many events. Because the specialist athlete has only a limited area to cover, he can do it intensively with a good chance of finding something with which to harass the coach. And when he does, he tries to make the fullest use of it. When he confronts the coach, he wants the confrontation to be conspicuous. He wants other listeners around.

Some "real" coaching / When I was a young coach, my coaching was not at its most sophisticated level, but it was quite intense. I remember working with a shot-putter whose prep school coach had had no understanding of the event. As a result, the youngster had acquired some habits that were both injurious and highly tenacious. Working with him to correct these habits was like pulling teeth. But slowly he began to improve. He started to acquire sound fundamentals, and his distance increased more than six feet. He had reached the point where he could score for the team. Spring vacation arrived, and he announced that he was going back to his old prep school to "get some real coaching and get straightened out." I was shocked. Some years later, I would not have been. After vacation he returned with his previous bad habits restored and a drop in performance of the same six feet he had gained under my tutelage. I don't know if I would have gone through the entire routine again, but I never had to find out. Some beginners in his event came along well and crowded him off the team.

The pattern of resistance is sometimes tricky to diagnose. In some instances the coach may not be highly competent in the athlete's event. The secure coach may recognize his own weakness and even help to arrange outside coaching. Actually, the athlete should eventually become steeped in knowledge about his event. His source of information should not be restricted to his own coach. Some of the athlete's information may, for example, come from the observations of top performers in his event. Nevertheless, the athlete who openly announces that he is turning to a different coach or to some other source is likely showing resistance bordering on hostility.

THE "PROBLEM ATHLETE"

More and more the expression "problem athlete" has been receiving wide currency. The athletes are responding by talking about "problem coaches." There may be validity on both sides, but in any case the phrase "problem athlete" could use a little examination.

An essential point that I've been hopeful of making is that anyone who seriously tries to change another person's deep-rooted behavior must expect to meet resistance. We compared the task of the coach to that of the psycho-therapist. The psychotherapist expects resistance from a patient. In fact, if he doesn't observe any resistance in the course of treatment, he is concerned that real progress is not being made. In contrast, the coach is usually constantly disturbed by resistance on the part of an athlete. Instead of accepting resistance to change as a natural, and perhaps essential, part of the coaching process, he prefers to join in the cry of "problem athlete." Unfortunately, the coach can be aided and abetted in maintaining this unrealistic and harmful position by the "psychological counselors" at his university. The counselor is usually a person who teaches a course or two but has as his *raison d'être* the dispensing of valuable advice. His chief tools are batteries of so-called personality tests. He administers the tests and then meets with the subject to explain the results. This process having been carried out, the subject is now considered aided. When the counselor gets into the sports field, he takes his *modus operandi* with him. If that's all he's got, he is not likely to do much good. To "test" the athlete and then offer the coach a prescription could very well obscure the psychology of the coaching task. But that's what the counselor seems to do. A "friendly counselor" is not in a position to understand the natural events that lead a coach to label an athlete a "problem." Faulty diagnosis is bound to be injurious.

Who are called "problem athletes"? / For some psychologists the problem athlete is anyone so designated by the coach. I have never seen anything in the literature to indicate that the coach's nomination was rejected or treated with skepticism. It might be refreshing for a psychologist to say, "Coach, there's nothing basically wrong with that boy. You have apparently made an error." Though the designation of "problem" is made by the coach, he usually has observational data that cannot be completely ignored.

In general, the problem athlete is one who causes the coach trouble and frustration by (1) giving him a hard time, (2) not performing up to his estimated potential, (3) showing decreased motivation, (4) presenting disciplinary problems, and (5) exhibiting bizarre behavior. No doubt there are even more symptoms than these. Any one or all of these patterns can be shown by the same athlete.

Most of the problem athletes who have come to attention via the publications are from the individual sports. There are a number of reasons for this. Team sports are usually unable to tolerate a problem athlete long enough to deal with him. Such an athlete tends to drop out, be ignored, or discarded. There is seldom room for him. The athlete who cannot conform to the team routine spells discomfort or trouble for the coach. Since there is very little quantitative measurement of performance in the team sports, an athlete of considerable physical potential can easily be overlooked if his "attitude" is unacceptable. Of course, the athlete of enormous potential is easily perceived. Even if he presents serious personality problems, the coach dare not dismiss him right away. This is the time when the coach may scurry around seeking professional help. However, by definition this type of extraordinary ability doesn't come along very often. More typically, the problem athlete is the one who has previously done well and then begins to perform poorly, or even quits. In general, in a team sport the problem athlete has to have readily perceivable potential or have shown past ability in order to receive attention. Otherwise, he is simply ignored or dismissed. Even if the potential great can be "saved," his effect on team morale has to be considered.

There is a great deal more room for the problem athlete in the individual sports than in team sports. To date, track and field has supplied most of the cases that have appeared in the sports psychology literature. Track and field has been an attractive research area, probably because (1) it is highly quantitative—performances are reliably measured to fractions of an inch and fractions of a second—(2) it has many individual skills that permit an examination of the learning process, and (3) track and field offers something of a sanctuary for the eccentric who likes to express himself in his own way. All the ingredients are there for a good look at athletic behavior.

Orientation of the athlete / Sometimes a problem athlete is one who has an orientation to sports that is simply different from that of the coach. The athlete may regard sports participation as a hobby, something he likes to do for fun. It is a rare coach who has a similar orientation. Instead, the typical coach expects discipline, conformity, and dedication on the part of the team member and assumes that the athlete will show these qualities. But suppose the athlete is not aware of these obligations.

The outstanding high school football player who has been recruited and paid by a large university should know the reality that confronts him. He should know what behavior is expected of him. But an athlete who goes out for an individual sport such as track and field may have no idea that he is joining a team and in this way incurring obligations. He may turn out for track simply because he likes to jump, run, or throw. Such an approach seems so naive that the possibility of its existence is seldom considered by the coach. Also, the teammates of such an athlete are likely to be conscious enough of the team and their duty to it to have little sympathy for his motivation. Actually, the emphasis on loyalty to the team produces effective performances. First, the athlete will tend to do better if he is conscious of competing as a member of a team. In this way he is much freer to express aggression. Second, the average athlete responds favorably to the network of commitments imposed by membership in a team. He is likely to train harder and make sacrifices for the good of the team.

But the athlete who doesn't know about the responsibilities he incurs when he joins a team is likely to become a "problem," especially if he performs well. I once coached one of the most conscientious youngsters I have ever known. He did about everything society asked of him. He seemed to be a model citizen in every way—he was polite, well mannered, well behaved. Though his academic aptitude scores were not outstanding, he was graduated first in his high school class. At college, he took a difficult premedical course because his family told him to. Yet he wasn't a rigid, compulsive person. He enjoyed life. He just believed in working hard and doing well. When I congratulated him on being elected to Phi Beta Kappa, he was somewhat apologetic, saying that he really wasn't very bright. He just worked hard. I pointed out that achievement requires no apology.

His one release from all his duties was his delight in the pole vault. The vault was his hobby or recreation— pretty much like stamp collecting or going fishing. His trouble began when he got very good at the vault. He started to clear fourteen feet, an excellent performance prior to the days of the fiberglass pole. Our championship meet was coming up, and we were going to be in a close battle to defend our title. He happened to mention to me that he would not be at the meet because he had committed himself to take a girl to the junior prom to be held the same night as the meet. There wasn't much I could do except try to orient him to a realistic situation that he should consider. His teammates were assuming that he would be on hand to contribute to the critical team effort. They had willingly and spontaneously given up attending the prom and would not have understood his going to a dance instead of to the all-important championship meet. If he failed to appear at the meet, he would be cold-shouldered from then on. Incredible as it might seem to most coaches, he never thought in terms of team effort. To him, the team was just a lot of nice people—he was fond of them, and they were fond of him—enjoying their pleasant hobbies. But now his own hobby changed into an obligation—and he had plenty of those already.

After much agonizing, soul searching, and painful conflict, he finally canceled his date for the prom and went to the championship meet. He failed to clear any height, and I guess that he never really enjoyed vaulting again. He stayed with the team, but his performances were poor. Vaulting had become one more responsibility in a life that was already packed with them. After college he went on to medical school and eventually graduated with honors. Was he a problem athlete?

A similar case is that of the runner who simply likes to run for the fun of it. He enjoys running and appreciates the physical and mental health benefits running gives, but he has no intention of letting the sport dominate his life. He relegates his running to what he deems an appropriate portion of his day-to-day existence. The coach, on the other hand, is familiar through his reading with the type of workout schedules that produce world-class performances, and wants to get the runner on a program that is used by the championship runner. If the runner has other interests in life, he may not be willing to undertake the fierce, all-out schedule of the greats, and although the coach knows the workout patterns of the greats, he may have many problems enforcing them on this athlete. The coach has his viewpoint and the athlete has his. There is a clash of orientations. The coach seldom tolerates or understands the pattern presented to him by this type of athlete. Similarly, the athlete is unlikely to change his orientation and take on a new set of values in order to accommodate the coach. The coach may think that the youngster needs a psychiatrist, but, of course, the pattern in itself is not at all evidence of pathology.

Mental health and the problem athlete / Like any of us, an athlete is susceptible to neuroses or psychoses. However, the layman usually makes his diagnosis of "crazy" on a basis that is different from the one used by a psychiatrist. Lack of understanding of a person usually comes from people who are completely dedicated to some pursuit. They are intolerant of an associate who is not similarly dedicated. Anyone who fails to share their dedication is suspected of having something wrong with him. This attitude is the product of strong egocentricity. But great achievement seems to require an unreasonable egocentric orientation. A combination of drive and an intolerance of the views of others seems needed. Such an orientation is prevalent in coaching, but it pervades nearly all areas of human activity, including business, the military, and education. Educators, for example, seem to hold it as an article of faith that mental health is directly related to the intensity of the academic effort. The almost unquestioned assumption is that if a student performs below par, i.e., gets grades lower than those his intelligence scores suggest he should get, he's got an emotional problem. After all, a beautiful and normal psyche should express itself in fine schoolwork.

Some years ago I had occasion to review hundreds of studies on the relationship between mental health and academic performance. The evidence, which I presented in a medical journal, indicated that all levels of mental health were represented throughout the academic spectrum. Normal and disturbed youngsters are found among both the poor and good students. There are many instances of schizophrenics achieving scholastic honors. I suppose an avid stamp collector might take the position that if all of us were straightened out mentally, we would devote our efforts to collecting stamps. Are we "problem" stamp collectors?

One of the weak aspects of sports psychology is that the psychotherapists who enter the athletic area seem unaware of the egocentricity of the coach. It's bad enough that they almost uncritically accept the coach's testimony concerning the behavior of the problem athlete, but even worse that they feel obliged to side with the aims of the coach. It is disturbing that a therapist can lose his perspective and naively become party to an attempted manipulation of the athlete. Of course, this type of effort is constantly made in other fields, especially in industry, but I think many of us shrink from the idea of this happening in sports. Yet we know from the publications that it is happening. There is little hard evidence that the psychologists have been effective, even though they report glowing results.

Identifying the problem athlete / It is important that we get back to the labeling of the problem athlete, because the research proceeds from that point. If this important link is of sand, all that follows is nonsense. The initial diagnosis of an athlete being a problem has to be valid. But judging from the published material, it seems that sports psychologists rely heavily or even completely on the coach to nominate the problem athletes. This approach on the part of the therapist is naive and surprising. I know of one prominent publication dealing with problem athletes where the coaches doing the labeling were technically incompetent. Politically oriented, the coaches survived by courting the right people. They had strong reason to be insecure in the face of a challenge by an athlete. Their ready defense was to label the offenders "problem athletes." I recall one published case in which the main complaint against the "problem" athlete was his belligerency toward the assistant coach. As it turned out, the assistant coach, now out of coaching, was found to be an absolute menace. Not only was he incompetent, he was a saboteur. He was constantly planting the suggestion that the athlete might be tired or that perhaps his old injury was coming back. In order to have any hope of success the athlete had to break contact with such a character. Under the circumstances "belligerency" seems a mild reaction.

Resistance to coaching, at least while behavior changes necessary to good performance are being effected, is a most healthy reaction. The athlete who shows initial strong resistance to coaching is almost certain to go much further than the compliant athlete. However, it takes a coach of perception and personal security to recognize resistance as the natural and benign reaction that it is. The unperceptive and insecure coach fails to understand coaching resistance no matter how frequently he encounters it. Every season he feels victimized by fate. He is surrounded by "problem athletes." It would be useful if he could keep in mind, painful though it may be at first, that yesterday's personnel hornet can be tomorrow's delight.

Most of the truly difficult problem-athletes probably go unrecognized. They are the athletes who show no verbal or other overt resistance to coaching. They listen to the coach politely. There is no backtalk, no direct challenge to the coach's security. But the athlete has the supreme resistance. He just doesn't change. He keeps the old habits that preclude improved performance. The coach's reaction tends to be: "A nice boy. It's too bad that he has very little ability." Who really knows?

The phrase "problem athlete" surely needs much more careful scrutiny. Definitions of the term ought to be realistic, useful, and clear. It's most important that we know what we are talking about, that we don't start out with hazy notions. The assumption that many sports psychologists bring to the field is that sports present a unique area where special problems pop up. There is the further suggestion that the behavioral expert can and should offer a corrective formula for the coach to carry out. At this point things begin to smack a bit of nonsense and even charlatanism. A good therapist or scientist should know better than to start prescribing remedies. If an athlete is designated as a problem, at least some specification is needed. A problem to whom? To himself? To society? To certain people? Often, it seems, an athlete is labeled as a "problem" simply because he aggravates and frustrates the coach. The use of the word "problem" can be invalid.

Surely we all have problems. Each of us is equipped with a nervous system which we use to mediate the environment. The environment is complex and so is the nervous system. The interaction between the nervous system and the environment is not going to be perfectly harmonious. A person without a problem of some sort would probably not be conscious. He'd be more like a vegetable. Problems are multiple and tend to be intertwined. However, for a professional therapist, the main problems are emotional ones that can bring personal misery and be disabling to normal lifetime pursuits. However, the correlation between personal misery and achievement can vary. A person with an extreme emotional problem may be capable of fantastic achievement. In fact, the irritant may be needed to bring about the achievement.

In brief, we could all be looked upon as "problem people." However, if we are not too miserable, not too dangerous, and able to get on with the everyday affairs of life, a competent therapist would probably say we were healthy and let it go at that. Some forms of psychoses may be discrete entities, but most of us would be classified at some point in a continuum of mental health. At one end of the scale we would be pronounced "well adjusted" and at the other end "poorly adjusted." So it is with athletes. It is sensible to remember that a person who becomes involved in sports does not discard his life story and personality. If his problems are difficult ones, they are likely to express themselves in the sports area, in part because that area is demanding. We can call him a "problem athlete," but that wouldn't seem to help matters. It would be more useful to call him a person with a serious emotional problem who is in athletics. Athletics, because of its strenuous and dramatic nature, may bring the problem into clearer focus. If so, the legitimate task of the therapist is not to please the coach but to help the athlete.

Who Will Do Well?

The selection of personnel for a team is, of course, always based on prediction. Candidates who look as if they will do well are selected, while others are rejected. Selection of squad personnel is one of the more critical tasks of the coach. Often, selection may be his most important job, as his ability to select can make the difference between success and failure. The coach and his staff can never be infallible, but they cannot afford to make more than their normal share of mistakes.

The efforts to identify those who will do well become more intense at each higher level of sports activity. The average high school coach comes to know the student body pretty well and can probably do a reasonably good job in picking the youngsters who are likely to be successful. His universe of prospects is limited. His mistakes can adversely affect the team record. His worst mistake, however, is to discourage some athletes who should be encouraged, for they may never again compete in sports. For the coach there is little intensity in the prediction process. His job is rarely at stake.

113

At the college level, the selection of athletes becomes a more intensive process, especially in football. The coach has a limited number of scholarships to offer and these must be distributed effectively. Mistakes can be highly costly to the coach's career. Losing coaches get fired. Usually college football coaches give much more time to recruitment of players than to actual coaching on the field.

At the professional level, the personnel selection effort is incredibly intense and thorough. A professional team can invest hundreds of thousands of dollars in a single athlete. It's understandable that they will pay for squads of scouts, miles and miles of motion picture films, and computer time in trying to decide whom to draft. The professional drafts are highly critical for the teams.

It seems certain that sports psychologists will become increasingly involved in the prediction of athletic performance. I would be hopeful that prediction efforts will not concentrate entirely on the development of empirical instruments. Research efforts are much more valuable to a science when they increase our theoretical understanding.

In any life story and with respect to performance in any activity, aptitude, personality, and happenstance interact to produce a result. Once an observable or measurable result has been obtained, we have a further base for prediction.

APTITUDE

The nature of aptitude / The term "aptitude" has been with us a long time, and because it has been used and ill-used so often, our definitions have become a little cloudy. But in general we can say that aptitude refers to the amount of innate ability or potential to perform well in a defined area. The use of the word "aptitude" presents many theoretical difficulties. First, of course, the term is an abstraction, and we have to make inferences about it from observed behavior. When we do so, our process may be circular and therefore not very helpful. If I say that Mozart had an aptitude for music or that Einstein had an aptitude for physics, I will be on very solid ground because I am making inferences from the enormous achievements of these two remarkable persons. But I would not be bringing you much news. I could make you yawn just as much by telling you that O. J. Simpson has aptitude for football and Pelé for soccer.

But our present efforts to assess are still largely circular. Our ultimate success perhaps hinges on whether we can gain significantly in our ability to predict. I don't think we can, judging from the way things are going now. Still, the tests can be useful by saving us time. They can supply a much shorter work sample than the normal world offers. If, for example, a child is tested for musical aptitude, we can get a quick idea of how well that child might do in the world of music. Our prediction might be somewhat better after the child has had several years of music lessons, but the test is quicker, and perhaps more kindly, especially if the violin is contemplated. A second-rate baseball player is all right. Even a poor pianist is welcome at a songfest. But the second-rate violinist can only offer torture.

Scholastic aptitude / Efforts at prediction have been gigantic in many areas of human activity. There are other significant areas, but prediction of the ability to do school-work has involved many millions of dollars and many thousands of research projects. It would seem highly useful for the sports psychologist to examine these long and intensive efforts.

During the early part of this century, educators in France became interested in the problem of children's differential abilities to do well in school. It was felt that some children did not have the innate ability to master the work; others did apparently have aptitude but were thought to be lazy. The task was to find a way to distinguish between these two classes of subjects. Binet devised test items that were appropriate to the abilities of various age groups. For example, there were items that could be passed by the average six-year-old but not by the average five-year-old. After testing, the "mental age" of a child could be assessed. A later touch was added, though not by Binet. If the mental age of the subject is divided by the chronological age, the result is a number that is called the intelligence quotient, or I.Q. Therefore, if mental age and chronological age are the same the I.Q. is 1.00, or, dropping the decimal point, one hundred.

It would seem that the original hope was to measure something that might deserve the name "pure intelligence." It didn't really work out that way. A useful definition of intelligence is hard to come by. Surely any such definition would have to relate to the functioning of the central nervous system—its potential ability to mediate the environment. However, the intelligence-testing movement has had an educational orientation. With the proliferation of tests the word "intelligence" began to be partially replaced by "scholastic aptitude." This change may have represented a slight advance, since it seemed to suggest a lessened degree of egocentricity among the educators. Probably true, even though the original goal became hazy.

More and more, the testing movement in education became empirical. Test items that failed to correlate with academic achievement were dropped, and those that did correlate with academic achievement were added. They were added only because they seemed to work well in increasing an empirical prediction. In this way we acquired a slightly increased practical improvement of prediction at the expense of theoretical progress. The measuring instruments have tended to become conglomerates, and we don't know what the scores really mean. There may have been what seems like a short-term gain, but the loss is a stifling of productive research. Let's suppose that in a given situation the product-moment correlation between aptitude tests and academic grades amounts to .50. That means the variance is .25, which leaves 75 percent of school performance unaccounted for. Naturally, this has made for a situation enticing to researchers. The thought was that schoolwork is the product of both intelligence and personality factors. Since we can already measure intelligence, all we have to do is identify and measure the relevant personality factors and thus greatly increase the accuracy of prediction. All in all, the thousands of research efforts along this line have yielded just about nothing. The great difficulty has been that intelligence or scholastic aptitude tests do not produce reasonably pure measures. The tests already reflect personality factors.

The search to identify aptitudes in the sports area / I am optimistic that research involved with seeking and identifying athletic aptitudes will yield much more of value than the research efforts in academic aptitude. I have two main reasons for this feeling of optimism. First, there is the opportunity to learn from a long and intensive history of academic aptitude testing and in this way avoid a number of pitfalls. Second, I think the entire structure under which sports performance takes place affords far better opportunities than the classroom for observation and measurement.

As research on sports aptitudes goes on, certain guidelines will be useful. I'd like to suggest a few which I think are useful, with the expectation that others who are interested in this area will contribute more important ones in the future.

Coaches and others who should know better often use the expression, "An athlete is an athlete." The phrase is not very helpful, but its meaning is clear enough. Athletic aptitude is regarded as a single factor. A person has a certain amount of this quantity. If the quantity is great, the individual can do almost anything in athletics. This single factor of athletic aptitude could express itself about equally in almost any sport, depending on circumstances and interest. This is the "big single muscle" view.

Even early in this century some psychologists began to disagree with the "big single muscle" view as it related to the abilities of mankind. In the area of intelligence the notion of a general intelligence was not completely dismissed, but scientists felt that specific intelligence or abilities had to be taken into account. There was the big "G" that could represent general intelligence. Then there were the various "S"s, which would indicate specific intelligences or aptitudes. Specific aptitudes correlate in varying degrees with "G." In a way, of course, the correlations are mathematical artifacts, but the idea is that there is a general factor that tends to pervade and tends to be related to the specifics. A very strong man is not likely to be equally strong in all muscle groups. Nevertheless, if we measure the strengths of his various muscles we would get significant correlations with his overall strength.

To summarize the above point briefly, sports psychologists should not fall into the trap that still lessens the effectiveness of the intelligence-testing movement. As the academic people found, the "single big muscle" notion had to be challenged in a search for specifics. The ways in which specific aptitudes do correlate will provide exciting insights and will lead to new research efforts.

It seems that we do need terms. We have the choice between familiar words and cold symbols, but we tend to choose the words. Psychology deals with words that are literary heritages, and so will sports psychologists. In sports the more common terms relating to ability are "coordination," "balance," "speed," "strength," and "endurance." These terms seem to have a practical descriptive value, but they have to be treated with caution if we are not to fall into semantic traps.

All of us have seen what appears to be the highly coordinated youngster who is graceful in sports activity. He contrasts sharply with the awkward youngster who stumbles over his own feet. It becomes tempting to generalize about "coordination" and say that if an athlete shows it in one sport he will show it in all sports. But then we see an athlete who is graceful in one sport move to another and look awkward. That doesn't mean that the term "coordination" should be thrown out as a possible dimension of athletic aptitude. It only means that the term needs examination.

Some years ago I was instrumental in getting a college freshman interested in the discus throw. He had about every character trait one could hope for—high intelligence, determination, leadership, sense of humor. But he did not seem big enough to become a great discus thrower. He wasn't fast. He couldn't jump. Yet none of these apparent liabilities prevented him from winning about everything in sight and making the U.S. Olympic team. Even I, his coach, was a bit baffled by his great performances. What was the ingredient that could account for his becoming a world-class performer? I finally decided that it was balance, because he always finished his turn with a catlike balance. One day on the field he wanted to measure his practice performance in his secondary event, the shot put. Since a tape wasn't handy, he tried to measure by putting one foot in front of the other. As he did so, he wobbled and almost fell down. If I had only seen him throw the discus my explanation for his great success would have been "excellent sense of balance." If I had only seen him try to measure his put, my evaluation would have been "poor sense of balance." I don't mean that "balance" is a useless term in exploring aptitude. It just has to be watched.

My feeling is that "speed" is a useful and fairly solid concept in diagnosing sports aptitude. For the moment, in an effort to simplify, let's consider only running speed. Obviously, running speed is vital to good performance in many sports, not only track but soccer, football, and basketball. The speed at which a man will move along will depend on the frequency and length of his strides. Running speed can be very precisely measured over a given distance. The measurement has both high validity and reliability. It correlates well with performance in many sports. The hard-bitten professional football scouts rely heavily on timed running speed. Forty yards seems to be the favorite distance. Running speed is probably very basic. It seems to be almost innate. It is surely less susceptible to modification than most other sports activities. Still, it ought to be further explored rather than simply accepted as a component of sports aptitude.

In any search for sports aptitude we will surely be dealing intensively with the general notion of strength. Some sports activities require extraordinary strength, weight lifting being an obvious example. We are in an excellent position to assess the strengths of athletes in some detail. We can even measure the strengths of the various muscle groups. We have the enormous advantage of knowing a great deal about the physiology of muscular strength. There is an obvious but curious aspect of physical strength. The person who is strong almost always looks strong. We can detect the person's great strength just by looking at his bulging muscles. And the person who is weak looks weak. In contrast, we can seldom say that the highly intelligent person looks intelligent. There are almost no surface clues. We need a performance in order to get any kind of measurement of intelligence. Even the great sprinter cannot look fast while at rest. He's got to run before we can measure him.

Having said some favorable things about physical strength as a promising aptitudinal element in sports, we find ourselves facing a difficulty. Strength can be greatly changed through exercise, especially progressive weight training. The changes can be remarkable. The athlete can, through weight training, add fifty or more pounds of muscle. He can double his lifting power and acquire a very different looking physique. Innate factors such as the number of muscle fibers and inherited body build will determine in important ways just how far the person can develop his strength. But researchers will have a difficult time separating innate strengths from acquired strengths.

The concept of endurance seems legitimate and offers promise in the search for aptitudinal factors in sports. Surely it is much less nebulous than most of the other elements that we have been considering. We know that endurance is almost everything to some sports, such as marathon running, and critical to many others. For example, it isn't enough for a soccer player or football player to acquire the skills of his game. He must also be able to last. The concept of endurance has attracted many ingenious physiologists. Their research has created a rich and useful literature. However, the sports psychologist faces the same problem here that he does in dealing with strength. Since endurance, like strength, can be greatly increased by modern training methods, its presence as an innate capacity becomes covered over and hard to detect.

The elements of aptitude / A person who is involved in what we recognize as science can emphasize either a theoretical structure or immediate and practical results. My own prejudice is that those who emphasize only practical results are not scientists at all, desirable as their results may be. They are technicians. They have some chance to benefit mankind, but very little.

We've spent some time looking at the intelligence-testing movement. I trust that it's not unfair to summarize by saying that it condemned itself to stagnation by concentrating on empirical instruments of prediction and by virtually abandoning theoretical thinking and research. If sports psychologists follow the same path, they are destined to suffer the same fate.

Right now it is possible to develop testing instruments that would have substantial predictive value for sports performance. Various measurements and performances can be assembled. Criteria of successful sports performance can be devised. All of it could be fed into a computer. From this process there would emerge empirical instruments with predictive values. Then we could go through the factor analysis routine which didn't do much for intelligence testing. I am not suggesting that all empirical instruments should be eschewed. My suggestion is that the mainstream of research ought to be along theoretical lines.

The elements of athletic aptitude ought to be specified as best they can with the view that further thinking and research will increase purification. Suppose we turn to basketball. There are, as you know, five players on a team. There are five different positions and each player has slightly different emphases on tasks and responsibilities. Yet, all five of the players have to have certain common skills. They all have to be able to dribble, pass, shoot, guard. Now suppose that we come up with aptitude measures of these functions. Further, let's suppose that the measurements are strictly isolated in terms of neuro-muscular equipment. Subject "X" and subject "Y" get identical aptitude scores. However, it happens that "X" is seven feet tall and "Y" is five feet tall. We know that "Y" isn't going to make it. We can further postulate that "X" and "Y" have the same neuromuscular abilities and the same height, but one of them has personality problems that interfere with his ability to play effective basketball. Like lack of height, personality dysfunction can disqualify a person completely. An additive system of scoring a test, which is the present method, does not pick up a component that could indicate disqualification. We see the additive process in use in other areas. College admissions officials are fond of using the multiple regression equation. The mathematical base currently used in predicting behavior surely has to be changed.

PAST PERFORMANCE AS A PREDICTOR

The best single predictor of behavior of almost any kind, in the present state of the art, seems to be past behavior projected into the future. Of course, to make use of this prediction method we have to have a past or present situation that resembles the future situation in which the prediction is to be made.

American university admissions officials have probably had the broadest experience with behavior prediction.

Efforts to improve the prediction of students' college grades have involved thousands of studies, many millions of youngsters, and many millions of dollars. Despite the long, intensive, and expensive history of aptitude testing, the secondary school record is still the best single predictor. Nevertheless, in order to be admitted to a first-rate college all applicants are required to take a scholastic aptitude test (S.A.T.) and a number of achievement tests. The three measurements most often used, then, are the secondary school record, scholastic aptitude scores, and scholastic achievement scores in various subjects. The aptitude and achievement scores are considered to be kind of even-steven for everyone. They tend to eliminate local peculiarities because the tests are administered and scored on a nationwide basis. They protect against a candidate getting high grades simply because his uncle is a member of the board of education. Admissions officials find that secondary school grades need to be tampered with, or "adjusted," as it is usually called. That's mostly because public high schools tend to give generously high grades, whereas the exclusive private schools have traditionally felt that students ought to get low grades. A number of multiple regression equations take account of the grouping into which a candidate's school falls. What the process really amounts to is an assessment of the school's situational similarity to that of the college.

If I've been late for an appointment with you nine out of ten times, you rather expect me to be late for the next one. I wonder if the academicians have gone far beyond such a simple proposition. Their apparent lack of curiosity is a bit surprising. They seem to settle for the empirical finding that there is a significant and useful correlation between secondary school grades and college grades. The correlation is attributable to the similarities between the two "problem boxes," a term that will be explained below. Both levels involve books, assignments, classrooms, reports, paper and pencil tests. Though presumably at different levels, the same subjects are taught—English, foreign languages, math, sciences. In brief, there are similarities between the secondary school and college situations. But the *dissimilarities* will supply the truly useful clues to our further understanding of the uses of prediction. We ought to examine the "problem boxes" in an effort to discover the significant differences between them.

My use of the term "problem box," which I borrow from the vocabulary of researchers experimenting with animals, probably needs some clarification. The words are used simply as a convenient symbol. As a sports example, let's take a look at the application of "problem box" to baseball. We might call minor league baseball Problem Box A and major league baseball Problem Box B. There are great similarities between A and B. Such factors as rules and equipment are identical. Performance based on A is predictive of performance in B. The players who do well in the minor leagues are the best bets to do well in the majors. But such predictions are far from surefire. Players with similar playing records in the minors often have different fates when brought up to the majors. Some succeed, others fail, even when they appear to be equally promising. I think we have a good chance of increasing both the accuracy of empirical prediction and our understanding of sports behavior through analyses of the differences between minor league and major league baseball. Surely there are important psychological differences. It is not enough to point out that the majors are tougher, that the pitching and batting are better. After all, some minor league players perform even better when they reach the majors.

A series or hierarchy of problem boxes exists in nearly all sports. Coming back to baseball, we have sandlot, Little League, high school, minor league, and finally major league. Performance in each problem box tends to have predictive value for the next to come. In the cases of a few extraordinary performers some of the problem boxes can be skipped. But for the most part baseball players travel the route of problem boxes—that is, as far as they can.

The prediction process becomes critical and tense when players are selected for the major leagues. At stake can be the success of the team, the investment of the owner, the career of the manager, and the jobs of the scouts. For the most part minor league players are selected on the basis of measured performance. However, an experienced and shrewd scout will look for strengths and weaknesses that are not directly reflected in the playing statistics. For example, a hitter with a high batting average may have a poor throwing arm.

You might think I am a bit obsessed by the notion of "problem box." But I think it has its value in developing research approaches. Let me try to clarify further what I mean about the comparison of adjacent problem boxes. I've suggested that the comparison of the structures of the boxes can yield clues for research that might improve both empirical prediction and understanding. Going back to the academic situation, we have said that the problem box of secondary school is somewhat similar to that of college. That's the basis for the predictions that we can make. Yet one important difference between the two situations is the degree to which direct supervision of the student is exercised. The high school student has parents who check up on him. The private school student is under the watchful eyes of the masters. But once the student goes off to college, there may be little or no supervision of his behavior.

There may be no one to see if he even attends classes. An important key to prediction may be the student's reaction to withdrawal of supervision. He may go on working as before or he may stop working altogether. The problem box picture suggests that it might be useful to direct research efforts toward identifying and measuring such internal controls as "superego" and "sense of responsibility."

The most significant difference between minor league and major league baseball may not lie in the players' higher levels of hitting, fielding, throwing, and running. The real difference may be in the psychological climate surrounding each. In contrast to minor league ball, the majors are marked by enormous pressure, big crowds, national television coverage, and newspaper publicity. The player who succeeds in the majors is universally recognized as a high-level athletic achiever. In brief, a comparison of the two problem boxes suggests that research should focus on personality factors.

We have to give attention to the astonishing prediction efforts of the professional football teams. In terms of intensity and effectiveness it's hard to find any group that can compare with them. They are surely miles ahead of the admissions people at any college or professional school. As always, the chief predictor is the subject's performance in the adjacent problem box, college football. But the professionals do not blindly accept a record made in the problem box of college football. If they are interested in a player they want to see him perform. Experienced observers pick up nuances that often are not reflected in the record.

In the case of big-time college football the problem box gets very close to that of professional football. Not only is the quality of play high, but the psychological climate becomes similar to that of professional football.

Pressure is intense. The crowds can be even bigger than those attending the pro games. Television coverage is often nationwide. A player who seems outstanding in the Big Ten, the Big Eight, or one of the other tough conferences has to get serious attention from the professionals. Though the professional scout still relies heavily on recorded performance in the problem box, he wants to be on hand to get more information. For example, he may find that a running back's fine rushing record is largely attributable to extraordinary blocking by his teammates. There may be a passer with a superb completion record, but the scout notices that he throws many "bloopers." They are caught only because some fine receivers are outbattling the defensive backs. The scout knows well, of course, that the fierce and fast defensive backs in professional football won't be outbattled so readily. The problem box is made more predictive by a closer look at the performances that are made in it.

The prediction of human behavior is usually uncertain, but that should be more a source of fascination than frustration. No matter what our approach to prediction, the proof of the pudding is our ability to do it. Science properly makes a distinction between empirical and theoretical research. My own prejudice is on the side of the theoretical, but I don't entirely decry the empirical. The trouble is that empirical predictions tend to get better to a certain point and then stop on a dime. They usually lead to a dead end, with no insights for further progress. On the other hand, it's possible for the pure theorist to be in touch with nothing real in this world. I look for the empirical researcher to do some original "impractical" thinking and for the theorist to consider what the empirical workers find.

A Pattern Named Desire

The young coach often begins his career on the banquet circuit with the inevitable inspirational speech about the importance of motivation or "desire." Usually he has received some help with the speech from the public relations chap at his institution. After he has coached a while, the young coach realizes, "My God! This 'desire' stuff really is important. It does work." The theme of the banquet speech becomes a vital reality. Sooner or later, every coach sees the incredible achievements produced by powerful motivation. The highly motivated athlete can often perform at a level far beyond the expectation of the coach. With extraordinary desire he who appears to have little physical potential often goes on to achieve outstanding success. Such a pattern is more likely to be seen in the quantitative sports like track and field and swimming. In the team sports, where evaluation of the athlete is subjective, an athlete who improves through great desire will have difficulty overcoming the early appraisal made of him. He is usually tabbed early in his career, and after that, recognition is hard to come by. To show his new abilities he may need a happenstance such as injuries to the personnel rated ahead of him.

On the negative side, a formerly great performer who has lost his desire to do well may be truly detrimental to team success. The prevailing evaluation of the athlete can be out of date. The tendency is to remember him at his best. But with diminished motivation he changes from an asset to a liability.

That complicated word "motivation" / Our assessments of motivational strength can seem at times disarmingly simple. Most of the time we feel a confidence in making a judgment of a person's approach to an activity on a scale somewhere between complete disinterest and enormous intensity of interest. The college dean can ask, "How motivated is this student toward his studies?" And there can be some kind of an answer, at least for a point in time. In one sense it seems practical to regard motivation as a quantity that can be measured in linear fashion.

To view motivation as a point on a scale instead of as a raw dichotomy of "Yes, he is motivated" or "No, he is not motivated" is at least something of an advance over the naive and primitive thinking we have seen in the past. But even assuming that we can assess degree of motivation with reasonable accuracy, the procedure is only good as a possible selection item. It does offer some help in picking certain candidates and eliminating others. But it does little to increase our understanding of desire as we try to nurture it or stimulate it.

One's motivation to do well in an activity is the complex product of many forces. Two athletes might have what seems to be about the same motivation for success, but the factors that have combined to make for an apparent equality of drive could have very different sources. The many pressures that make up a kind of totality that we call "motivation" can include the conscious and the unconscious. A force can be subtle or simple. Some of the forces that determine the final product of motivation can be in conflict with each other. It might seem strange, but psychiatrists know that it is common enough for a person to have a strong drive to do well in a certain area and along with it a strong drive not to do well in the same area. Does that make sense? It should to a lot of us—especially the football coach, if he thinks about it. The football coach knows that, at any one time, position is the result of both offensive and defensive action. In other words, the ball's position on the field is the product of conflict. So too is motivation the product of conflict.

Any discussion of motivation has to be naive and therefore limited if it does not take account of the complexities that psychiatrists and psychologists have discovered. Any discussion of human behavior eventually has to come to grips with the term "motivation" in some form or another, even if badly understood. But, to avoid semantic difficulties and confused and unproductive thinking as best we can, we must avoid a simplistic and futile approach to this important topic. Still, we must approach it.

The shifting base / The motivation for play activity changes with increased maturity—or maturation if you prefer to think in physiological terms. A kitten plays, scampers, and engages in mock combat. The older cat never plays. He moves when he has to, most always in response to organic needs. The old tiger no longer frolics. A short time ago, I filmed the physical education activities of three primary school classes—first, third, and fifth grades. Every single youngster, including the ones with physical disabilities, performed with great outputs of energy and enthusiasm. Because of their enormous efforts, I thought it best to give them rest breaks. But their idea of rest breaks was to put out even greater energy in other play activities. Now, let's take another look at the same school system at a different level. Keep in mind that we are talking about the same town and the same socioeconomic group. Consider the high school level. As we move to that level, there is a puzzling drop in physical activity among the students. They show more than indifference. They show strong avoidance. They will find pretenses to avoid gym classes and, if need be, will bring in medical excuses from friendly family physicians. Why this drastic shift from delight in physical activity to detestation of it? Possibly much could be done by imaginative physical educators, but they may be fighting something basic enough to be difficult. There may be a diminishing of the physiological cues that trigger play activities. It may be that at the high school level the growth needs are partially satisfied and the chemical cues to great bodily activity are lessened.

If we can assume that in the early stages of life there is a strong tendency of the organism to exercise strenuously and perhaps aggressively, and if we can further assume that exercise tapers off with more physical growth, then two useful questions arise: (1) What sports will be seized upon as the early outlets for physical activity? (2) Under what conditions will the original physical and emotional output be sustained or even increased?

Early factors / The youngster's athletic activity tends to center on a particular sport or a few sports. And such an attachment is likely to continue throughout an athletic career. No athlete is innately destined to embrace a particular sport. The choice will be largely determined by a combination of cultural and geographical factors. Happenstance will also play a part in individual cases. A youngster growing up in Canada will be more inclined to turn his attention to ice hockey than someone growing up in the Upper Sudan. But even within similar geographical areas, different cultural and psychological climates exist for the various sports. The city ghetto produces fine basketball players and nearly all of the great boxers—but no cricketers or polo players. The ghetto has not produced good swimmers. It can be pointed out that there are not many pools in the ghettos. But the ghetto has consistently produced many of the finest trackmen in the world, and there aren't many tracks there either.

In many parts of the United States the youngster from the suburbs is fiercely motivated toward hockey. He'll undergo almost any hardship to attend practices and games. If the only available practice time is at three, four, or five A.M., he will still be on deck and ready to go. In the same suburban areas why isn't a similar drive shown, for example, toward participation in soccer? We can't say that hockey is intrinsically more exciting than soccer. Worldwide, soccer engenders more excitement and enthusiasm than does any other sport. For every single highly motivated young American hockey player there are hundreds of youngsters throughout the world who have the same excitement about soccer.

A comparison of the status of American football with that of soccer in the United States demonstrates the overwhelming influence of culture in determining sports interests. The impact of football, especially professional football, on the American public is utterly fantastic. Watching professional football on television involves most of the nation. It's a weekend way of life. No other television program can compete with it. Some years ago astronauts were making a historic, mind-boggling circling of the moon. The voyage surely had to be the equal of those of Columbus and Magellan. The network telecasting a professional football game briefly interrupted the game to bring a live telecast from the spaceship. The network's switchboards were quickly flooded with protests from the enraged fans. As for soccer, its impact in Europe and South America is even greater than that of football in the United States. Soccer games have occasioned riots, assassinations, and suicides.

Soccer is the major sport in nearly every nation on earth, and yet efforts to transplant the game to the United States have fallen short of total success. A full-scale effort to set up a professional soccer league failed to the point that the teams were dissolved. At the present time, the best players in the United States have low salaries, although they are increasing. In contrast, Pelé of Brazil in his prime received millions of dollars and is a national hero in his home country. As many as two hundred thousand people have turned out to get a glimpse of him at an airport.

American attempts to transplant our style of football on European soil, dating back to the thirties, have been dismal failures, and these efforts seem to have been discontinued. But the efforts to make soccer a popular spectator sport in the United States are constantly being renewed. So far, the greater part of the audience seems to be made up of immigrants. If the efforts to make soccer an important part of the American sports culture do work out, the entire process should be of interest not only to athletic coaches but to social scientists.

Prestige and the coach / The prestige of a sport is closely related to its attraction for a student. Therefore, for the coach the prestige of his sport is important. The coaches at a particular school have a common interest in raising the prestige of sports in general. But at the same time, the sports at a school are competing with each other to attract a share of the available athletic talent. Most athletes will turn toward the prestige sports. The prestige of a sport depends on a number of factors. The most important ones will be tradition, the facilities given over to the sport, and the personality and efforts of the coach. The coach has to operate in ways that draw attention to his sport. The task is to make the sport attractive not only to potential candidates but also to the student body in general. Attendance and support from peers are needed. The coach's imagination may be as important as his technical competence.

A bad mistake many coaches make is the attempt to lie low during an unsuccessful season. The coach wants to hide until things blow over. He tries to eliminate or reduce publicity and the publication of the scores of the team's games, waiting for better days. The trouble is that such action tends to keep things from getting better. The team can be almost forgotten. Attention is lost that will be difficult to regain.

Though the athlete's perception of the prestige of his sport is highly correlated with the number of people who follow that sport, there still can be a kind of intensive prestige produced by a relatively few people who really matter to the athlete. Cross-country running can serve as an example of this process, with the caution that distance running may have a psychology unto itself. At most cross-country meets there are few spectators. Often, only the coaches and officials are there to watch. To the extent that the cross-country runner needs approbation for his strenuous efforts, it has to come from a small group of knowledgeable followers of the sport. And that may be enough for the runner.

Not many coaches will ever coach a crew, but coaches

can look at crew as a clinical example of the complications of prestige. As in cross-country running, recognition of performance comes from a small and closely knit group. The sports "authorities" in your local tavern can reel off endlessly the names of greats and near-greats in baseball, football, and basketball. But if asked to name one great crewman they would be completely stumped. There is not only the obvious anonymity in crew, but there is also a need for complete uniformity in action. Each crewman must pull in precisely the same rhythm as the others. An individual burst of enthusiasm would be disastrous. A crewman seems to be in the tradition of the galley slave who is chained to his oar. So it does seem curious that crew became, at least for a time, the sport of the aristocracy of America. Did this come about through guilt or the parental feeling that stern discipline is needed for the offspring? In any case the personal prestige of an oarsman was mostly limited to the tiny universe of certain families. These families, during the high noon of crew, were known to each other. They were united by social bonds. The high noon of the Ivy League crews could exist only as long as the tradition that a son had the right to flunk out of his old man's college. In the old days there were always plenty of candidates for crew, and they all showed up for practice even before the ice on the river had melted. The crewmen needed no excuses. But with the great premium placed on secondary school performance by Ivy League admissions officials, the sons of first families started to be crowded out. There came a great influx of middle-class students, most of them lacking any tradition of crew.

Another word about prestige / As a person matures, sport is not used primarily to satisfy organic drives, as it is when he is young. A shift occurs from physiological drives to the need for prestige. The ancient Greek champions received wreaths of laurel. The laurel surely had no monetary value. The champions could have gone out in the woods and picked the laurel themselves. The prestige was the thing. At the outset of a career in sports various drives become important, including the organic ones. Later on, especially after outstanding achievement has been realized, additional motives enter the picture. But the prestige drive is always there. Sometimes the prestige drive is apparent and at other times it seems to be obscured by other needs.

The child's first impulses toward play and sports activities do appear to be largely physiologically based, but it does not take long for the prestige aspect to appear. The child does want recognition for any sports prowess that he's developed. Later on, as the physiological base for sports activity becomes less important, social factors become more important. At some stage of the game, perhaps high school and early college, the prestige drive is clearly seen. Even when we get to the professional level of sports, where money appears to be the obvious consideration, the prestige drive remains important. If you could set up an experimental situation in which the professional athlete was assured of top salary but was never to be mentioned in the media, he would be most unhappy. He might not survive. The professional surely won't perform without the money, but he still wants the prestige.

Money quickly becomes linked with prestige. The salary that a professional athlete can command becomes a measure of his prestige. The change from amateurism to professionalism seems abrupt, and it is irreversible. Every football player has started his career without monetary compensation. But if he is paid one way or another, e.g., by athletic scholarship, he will never play again unless he is paid. The trackman may struggle to get his entry accepted by a prestigious meet and pay his own way to get there. But once he is paid "expenses" he won't ever run again without being paid.

The emphasis here on prestige or recognition as a motivating force may seem extreme. It may appear that the satisfaction of achievement is in itself a sufficient reward. Of course, there is a personal satisfaction in sports achievement. A golfer who breaks ninety for the first time will feel elated. But doesn't he also want to tell somebody about it?

The dropout / We have to consider the dropout because in most sports situations dropping out represents an extreme loss of motivation. At the high school level, the physiological needs of those who drop out of sports may be similar to those who stay. The great difference lies in success. The star athlete is acclaimed by his school and his town. The poor sports performer gets no prestige from his participation and leaves his sport to seek recognition elsewhere. He may turn to another sport, the school newspaper, or to dramatic productions. And, of course, he may look for prestige in activities away from the school scene, some of them producing unfortunate results.

In college there is also a dropout pattern, but it may occur at a more complicated level. Nearly every realistic candidate for a varsity college squad has had considerable secondary school success. He has usually been all-something or other. Each high school star has developed a possible asset. Perhaps we can call it an "ego resource." Even after the original motivational base has disappeared, the resource remains. Under what conditions will the resource be used? It will be used when it proves to be a true resource by yielding gains. The potential gains are prestige and money. The two are intertwined. In nearly all colleges the successful athlete can get both prestige and a "free ride." There can, however, be situations at an Ivy League college where some members of a team get no financial help. Prestige has to keep them going. But most good college teams are made up of paid athletes, and completely so. Lincoln once said that the nation cannot exist half slave and half free. An athletic team cannot exist half paid and half amateur. Money is not only nice in itself; it also becomes a form of recognition. The unpaid athletes will drop out even if they don't need the money.

It seems easy enough to understand why an athlete of limited ability drops out. His resource is just not strong enough to produce satisfactions, and it has to be abandoned. The coach is pleased enough to see such candidates leave the squad; he is saved the unpleasant task of cutting them. But the coach is bewildered and upset when an excellent performer quits. There could be any number of reasons for an outstanding athlete to drop out. Let's consider a few patterns that seem to be in line with the theme that prestige is often the key factor in persuading an athlete to stay on.

Prestige may not be as obvious as it seems to be. We have to know the source of prestige and its meaning. If an athlete gets enormous publicity in the media, it's easy to assume that he is enjoying a feeling of great prestige. But this may not be so. We have to know the athlete's world. His important world may consist of a relatively small number of people. The really important world to the athlete could be made up of roommates, fraternity brothers, or others who have influence over him. His feelings of prestige may be almost totally centered on a relatively small number of people. Their reactions are really what matter. If they clearly take pride in the athlete's achievements, his motivation to perform well will be reinforced. But things could go in the opposite direction. The

athlete's world, even though the members may secretly
envy him, can diminish his motivation. The people close
to the athlete may constantly pressure him to do "something worthwhile—something intellectual." The athlete
may be constantly bombarded with the jibe "When are
you going to mature and stop being just a dumb jock?"
His group can very well get to him. If they do, his athletic
effort may diminish greatly or he may quit outright. It
takes an unusually perceptive and sensitive coach to be
aware of such a situation.

Another dropout pattern is also involved with the
prestige drive. A great performer can actually lose prestige
if sports are all that he can do. He may have to do
something more—like play a musical instrument, sing, be
involved in campus politics, or attain academic honors. A
great athlete with no other achievement can be regarded as
"only a jock." Some athletes won't know or care what
people think of them. But the sensitive athlete who feels that
his sports achievements are only diminishing his prestige
may quit.

The athlete who participates in two or more sports is
also likely to drop out, and do so in such a way that would
puzzle the coach. An athlete who is a star in two sports is
likely to continue with them both. But if he becomes
outstanding in one sport and remains only fair in the
other, he will probably quit the sport in which he is only
fair. Let's suppose that the athlete is a second-string
quarterback on the football team and a reasonably good
all-round weight thrower on the track team. Now, if he
becomes the star quarterback, and, at the same time,
another weight man reduces him to number two on the
track squad, we can be almost certain that the successful
quarterback will not report for track. That's because his
prestige, gained by being a top football player, can only be

reduced by being a second-string man in track and field. By way of gaining further prestige he can do better by being known as almost anything else, including a socialite.

Are there other motives that make for achievement? / Of course! Every experienced coach has seen an athlete who drives ahead regardless of the playback that he gets from his environment. Often the driving force is unconscious and unknown to the coach. Yet, such cases are relatively rare, and there are likely to be complications if achievement reaches a high level. The athlete who drives ahead with relentless motivation often is plagued by injuries and unexpected critical mistakes. We live in a society in which most of the basic drives such as hunger, thirst, and shelter are reasonably well satisfied. As a result, other less organic or basic drives become promoted. In some parts of our culture prestige may now be one of the important motivations. The prestige drive is a guideline for understanding the behavior patterns of many athletes. It cannot account for everything, but it can help supply a frame of reference for both prediction and perhaps a certain amount of control.

Regression
Under Stress

The phrase "regression under stress" means simply that when a person is under pressure he goes back, or regresses, to an earlier level of skill. Athletic competition produces stress, with the result that the skill level of an athlete tends to drop. Sports competition simulates warlike or emergency conditions, and the body responds by going into a warlike or emergency state. The sympathetic division of the autonomic nervous system becomes dominant. Pulse rate and blood pressure increase. Breathing is faster, and the sweat glands are more activated. Actually, these are the very responses measured by a lie detector. Because the sympathetic nervous system is stirred up, the body is stronger and prepared for powerful efforts. But simultaneously there is a reduced skill level.

Let's consider a simple example. Suppose a person has started to take lessons in one of the sophisticated methods of self-defense. Let's further say that he has been trained in some of the protective moves. Now, presume he is actually attacked on the streets. What will he do? We can't predict in detail what the reaction will be. The physical situation and personality factors will be determinants. If he can, he'll probably run. But if he is cornered and forced to fight, we can predict two things. First, he will be stronger than usual. Second, he will regress to a point prior to his self-defense training. The chances are that he will flail out wildly at his attackers. But with further training his defense will be more orderly and effective.

We may find another example of regression under stress in the javelin thrower. The average javelin thrower moves into throwing position by first running and then taking a hop. The great throwers, however, run into and through a more basic power position. Both the coach and the athlete realize that the hop must be discarded in favor of a more effective technique. Hence, practice time is devoted to making the needed change. Progress in practice is made. But in competition the thrower reverts to the hop. Under pressure he returns to an earlier stage. The hope is that one day he may not regress.

In general, under the stress of competition the organism is stronger than it is in the practice situation, but skill is reduced to a somewhat earlier level. Accepting this proposition, we find that the effects of stress will depend upon the nature of the athletic event. Most athletic events involve both strength and skills. The ratios differ. For the various sports strength can be nearly all-important or there can be a greater premium on skills or techniques. For example, weight lifting, though it does have its techniques, places an enormous premium on strength. Pitching in baseball represents a middle ground. Both power and accuracy are needed. A pitcher who can throw with great power cannot survive if he is unable to control the direction of the pitch. But he would not survive either if he simply had control without power. At the other extreme from weight lifting we have some athletic efforts that for practical purposes require no power at all: putting in golf or shooting foul shots in basketball, for example. It's hard to get good data on the golfer making his putts, mostly because the greens vary from course to course, However, in basketball foul shooting the conditions are standard. The foul shots are completely unopposed. Hence, success is a matter of the increase of accuracy under stress conditions. One famous basketball coach, who compulsively kept precise records, found the following: In practice free throws were made 78.0 percent of the time, while in games the completion figure dropped to 59.8 percent. Clearly, stress reduced accuracy.

It seems reasonable to expect that in nearly all sports the athlete will show both regression and greater power under game conditions. In tennis the service will be hit with more zing but with less accuracy. In football the block will be harder but made with less use of the best technique. In wrestling, holds will be made or broken with greater strength, but with less skill and more vulnerability to countermoves.

To summarize briefly, the stress situation of competition produces greater strength but a regression in skill level. What action is indicated on the parts of the coach and athlete to counteract this phenomenon? The answer seems simple enough—overlearn! Practice the skill over and over again. It's repetition and overlearning that will do the job. We can expect the skill level to be reduced in the stress situation. But with intensive practice, even though there is regression under competitive conditions, the form pattern to which the athlete will regress can still be highly effective.

Stress is needed in competitive sports in which strength

is an important factor. In such sports the athlete can do better under competitive stress than he can in the practice situation. There are exceptions which we will be talking about later. However, the average athlete becomes stronger under stress. His form still suffers. It's a matter of how much. The coaching goal is to make "backup form" so good that when the athlete reverts to an earlier stage his form is still solid. We have no way of generalizing on the time factor in regression. Under stress the athlete could be pushed back weeks or years. The greater the stress the further back he is likely to go. Overlearning over a long period of time makes a critical difference. Under stress the experienced athlete tends to do the "right thing" when the chips are down. Even in a regressive state he can perform well.

The pattern of regression under stress has important implications for the coach and athlete. As the major competitions draw near, the introduction of changes in techniques should be avoided as much as possible. Of course, improvements in form are needed for progress, but radical changes should be introduced only very early in the season, or, even better, during the off-season. At the peak of the competitive season, it would seem best for the athlete to polish the techniques that he already has and to maintain physical condition. A change in technique may seem to work well in practice, but it is not likely to hold up during the stress of competition and may even damage other techniques the athlete has perfected earlier.

Curiously, the highly talented athlete may be the one most adversely affected by late changes of techniques. If the competitive situation is stressful enough he is likely to regress, but at the same time retain something of what he has recently learned. He could be in the middle between two form patterns and come out with a poor performance. Let's take the case of a quarterback who generally performs well at his position but throws only a reasonably good pass. The coach concentrates on the athlete's passing technique. Perhaps he changes the position of the player's fingers on the ball and his arm action. The results in practice may look good, but in the actual games the quarterback can be caught between a partial regression to his old passing form and an implementation of some parts of the new form. The result could be a series of poor passes, including some bloopers that are easily intercepted.

Sometimes during the height of a season a football coach will introduce new formations and plays. Such tactics can surprise the opposition and often throw them off balance. But they also induce errors in execution. The record suggests that the most successful teams are those that carry out their "bread and butter" plays—the ones they practice and carry out in the games.

The above discussion should not be mistaken as a plea for a conservative attitude in teaching sports techniques. New approaches have to be tried. But in so doing we should take account of the realistic pattern of behavior that we can call regression under stress.

Retroactive Inhibition

During the early part of this century, psychologists paid much attention to learning problems. Using human subjects, they carried out countless studies in the psychological laboratories. In their efforts to formulate learning theories they felt it was necessary to explore both the conditions that facilitate learning and those that interfere with the learning process. From the great mass of early published studies in the area of learning, I think there are findings that have relevance for present coaching procedures. I am particularly struck by a pattern that was called "retroactive inhibition."

The idea of retroactive inhibition is easily understood. Suppose task A is learned to a certain level of acceptance. Afterward, task B is learned. Now we go back and check to see how well the learning of A has been retained. Interestingly, we find that the extent to which B interferes with the retention of A depends on the degree to which the two tasks are similar. If B is very similar to A there is likely to be great interference. If the two tasks are dissimilar there is practically no interference. We can understand this pattern operating in everyday situations. For example, it is easier to memorize two poems that are unlike each other than two that are similar. In the latter case we tend to get mixed up.

When I was a youngster in high school putting the twelve-pound shot, a coach suggested that if I switched to the sixteen-pound shot for a few weeks I would get a surprise. I did get a surprise. When I went back to the twelve-pound shot I could not put it as far as I could before. One of our Olympic hammer throwers spent most of his practice time working with an eighteen-pound hammer. When he went back to the standard sixteen-pound hammer, he found that for a time he couldn't throw it much farther than he had been throwing the eighteen-pounder. Weight throwers continue to practice with implements that are heavier than the standard ones. Even the high jumpers are attaching weights to their bodies. In the on-deck circle many baseball players swing several bats or a weighted one before stepping to the plate. However, in this case the effort is not to build strength but rather to create a subjective feeling that the bat is lighter.

The rationale for using heavier-than-standard implements prior to competition seems to be as follows. Strength has proven to be essential to most athletic events. Therefore, while the athlete is practicing his event, why not build up extra strength at the same time? Also, when the athlete returns to the standard weight implement it will feel light. Let's consider both of these reasons. By adding a few pounds to the implement the athlete is not building up much strength. Compare the above extra few pounds with weight-training exercises that involve hundreds of pounds. In brief, strength building can be carried out by much more effective means than adding weight to an implement. As for the subjective feeling of lightness, it is not very helpful. It is better for the shot to feel heavier but travel farther. For the batter it's better for the bat to feel heavier and get more hits. In summary, the subjective feeling that the implement is lighter is an illusion that interferes with performance.

The point is that a heavier implement changes the event slightly—just enough to cause learning difficulties. Putting the standard sixteen-pound shot is very similar to putting a twenty-pound shot. But the two tasks are not identical. To use our symbols, putting the sixteen-pound shot becomes task A and putting the twenty-pound shot becomes task B. If the techniques for putting both shots were precisely the same, no harm would be done by practicing with a twenty-pound shot. We would just have an interesting diversion in the workout program. However, that's not the case. Putting a heavier shot requires slightly different techniques. As a result, task B interferes with task A—the prescribed job of putting the sixteen-pound shot in competition.

Curiously, a strong case can be made for using *under-weight* implements in practice. Because of the stress situation the average athlete will actually be stronger in competition. This extra strength could actually change the event for the athlete. In a certain sense the shot-putter, if charged up enough in competition, is then actually putting an underweight shot for all practical purposes. And there is the possibility that practice with an underweight shot might be a good preparation for competition. An even stronger case for using underweight implements in practice can be made for the high school youngster who is rapidly gaining in size and strength. In high school competition the shot weighs twelve pounds. When the youngster starts his training, he adjusts to the task of putting twelve pounds. However, he is adjusting to a task that won't be appropriate as his size and strength increase. Ideally, he should start with a very light shot and gradually increase the weight of the shot as his strength increases. In that way the task could be kept nearly constant, and there would be a minimum of retroactive inhibition.

As far as I know, no responsible coach has ever proposed that basketball players practice with overweight basketballs or that quarterbacks throw an overweight football. If he has not, it speaks well for his coaching instincts. But if any coach tried such a procedure, most of the players would reject it. They would know almost instinctively that their timing and skills would be impaired. As for the baseball players, apparently they are both naive and instinctual about the use of an overweight bat. They don't actually use it to hit a ball, which is to the good. Just swinging an overweight bat before actually batting probably doesn't do too much harm, but there is a theoretical reason to think it may do a little harm. And in a game where close percentages can make the difference between victory and defeat, the possibility of even a little harm has to be avoided.

Any coach who tries to combine technique training and strength training should give some thought to the notion of retroactive inhibition. But sometimes the combined objectives can be realized fairly effectively, depending upon how similar the tasks are. For example, in football the sled may be a good device. Like the defender, the sled offers resistance. The blocker gets training in driving hard and builds up his strength. In the early stages the two objectives of developing a sustained drive against an opponent and building strength are somewhat compatible. But the reality is that a defender does not behave like a sled. The defender may have all manner of actions that the blocker has not encountered in sled training. So, work on the sled becomes an effective training and conditioning exercise but does not produce much retroactive inhibition. The sled is mainly a conditioning apparatus. Even though it is intended to simulate game conditions, it is removed from the real skill of taking care of a defender.

The pattern of retroactive inhibition can be considered part of the larger area known as transfer of training.

Transfer of training is concerned with the effects of learning in one area upon learning in other areas—i.e., the carryover value of learning. The early psychologists were intrigued by the problem of transfer and devoted enormous efforts to it. Much of the impetus for this great interest came from the centuries-old assumptions of the academicians, who predicated the school curriculum on the basis of "faculties." For example, Latin was not really included just so that students would know Latin. Its purpose was to discipline the mind. So it was with other subjects like mathematics and English. In general, selection of subjects for school and college programs was based on their assumed possible transfer values rather than their specific contents. They still are. Witness the commencement addresses of college presidents.

The literature on transfer of training is complicated and susceptible to many fascinating interpretations. Even after all these years of research, the problems associated with transfer of training have not been resolved. However, we know that the confidence in training for itself that directed the old academicians was naive. There is surely such a process as transfer of training, but it can be negative as well as positive. Retroactive inhibition is the prime example of negative transfer.

For the use of the coach and the athlete a valuable guiding principle emerges. Training in techniques and strength building should be kept separate.

Role Playing

Some psychologists feel that role playing holds the key to much of our understanding of human behavior. The trouble is that role playing seems to be a very difficult area to attack experimentally. As of now, we know that there are many unanswered questions, but we can be sure that the role that a person takes on will control a great deal of his behavior. The banker will behave in certain ways simply because he has assumed the role of banker. And so it is with the policeman, the college dean, the bricklayer, the athletic coach, the psychologist, etc. There are thousands of possible roles.

Eventually, role becomes tied in with occupation. When you meet an adult, you feel you know something about him just by finding out his occupation. One's major life role has to come with maturity and the selection of a career. The student's more permanent role is to be formed later in life. He will, however, take on early roles which tend to be related to campus activities.

To be successful the athlete must take on the role of athlete. Of course, the role of athlete in general won't do the job. The role has to be specific. The athlete has to think of himself as a lineman, a quarterback, a pole-vaulter, a discus thrower—that is, he has to identify with a specific event.

An enormous difference in effective behavior exists between the pole-vaulter and the student out for the pole vault. The pole-vaulter works out in the rain. The student out for the vault does not. The pole-vaulter makes personal sacrifices to get to practices and the meets, and in so doing is seldom aware that he is making any sacrifices at all. The student out for the vault will give up a practice session if there is something else he would prefer to do on a given day.

It would be useful if we knew more about how an athlete adopts or fails to adopt a role. This would make a most fascinating area of investigation for the growing number of sports psychologists. At present, however, I think we can make some guesses—they might even be called hypotheses because of the observations and experience that we have.

Certainly, if a young person is to assume the role of athlete in a particular sport, he or she must be exposed to that sport, and the circumstances of the exposure are important if not entirely critical. The enormous and excellent coverage of sports by television is surely producing some interesting results. We are now bombarded, pleasantly I think, by top-level performances in nearly all sports. And there are the human interest stories and various interviews of athletes which make the competitors identifiable. Baseball has ceded some of center stage to professional football, which is currently the biggest television sports attraction. But other sports are getting increased exposure. Youngsters can now see basketball, ice hockey, tennis, track and field, gymnastics, wrestling, skiing, weight lifting, auto racing, swimming. For a time boxing was writing itself off in favor of instant great profits via closed-circuit television. It may eventually fade away as a sport.

This intensive exposure to sports is bound to create fantasies in children. In their imaginations they used to be Superman. Now they are great athletes. As you observe youngsters in the playgrounds, you can see them living out their identifications with quarterbacks and wide receivers. Their knowledge of television terminology is striking. In their daydreams they are also stars of other sports. The fantasies pile up.

The first confrontation between fantasy and reality may occur early, especially in the suburbs where there is likely to be Little League Baseball, Pee-Wee Hockey, Age-Group Swimming, various football teams. By statistical definition the majority of the candidates can't cut the mustard and are either dropped or find it best to retreat. But for most youngsters the confrontation of their fantasies with reality comes in junior or senior high school when they try out for a team. It's then that they are apt to be bruised psychologically rather than physically. It is in this milieu that the coach can have his finest hour. When a youngster's athletic fantasies are smashed, the coach can exercise sensitivity. The youngster should not have his world come tumbling down. If there is no reasonable chance of his making a varsity squad, there may be a way that he can play with an intramural team—and always with the hope that one day again he can try for the varsity. It is my prejudice that the coach who handles this situation with sympathy and understanding makes a great contribution.

Let's take the case of a youngster of 120 pounds who had his heart set on being an all-pro lineman. In trying out for his high school team, he simply gets smeared. The busy coach could easily dismiss the youngster, but suppose the coach or one of his colleagues can find the time and interest to work a bit more. The disappointed athlete might find a niche in a sport where body weight is not important, perhaps golf, tennis, or distance running. The introduction of the athlete to a sport that is not included in his prior fantasies is critical to the acquisition of a new role. If the coach shows enthusiasm it will tend to be contagious. The neophyte should get to know the history and traditions of his new sport. Whenever possible he should see top-level competition. He should have opportunities to exchange views and form friendships with others in his sport. In general, the procedure of opening up new role-playing possibilities to a youth should amount to a favorable introduction and then increasingly deeper immersion in the sport.

Much has been said and written about pressuring children into participating in the various programs organized for them. For the most part this practice seems to be regarded unfavorably by social scientists and physicians. It's a difficult business to assess. In swimming, for example, the work load appears incredible. The children swim more mileage than the mature champs of yesteryear. They certainly do well, as is shown by remarkable performances, including world records set at about the time they reach puberty. But the dropout rate is high. We constantly read about the retirements of world-class teenagers. How is the role of swimmer lost at such an early age? Could it be the role was that of the parents rather than the child?

Role playing should be appropriate to a person's realistic position in life. With increased age it's necessary for good adjustment that old roles diminish in strength and new roles become stronger. It won't do for a man in his fifties to retain a prime role of pole-vaulter. Though a sustained interest in the athlete's old sport is salubrious, other roles in life should become dominant. An embracing of the role of athlete in a specific event is a powerful and necessary force in reaching potential achievement. But the role of athlete is really for youth—alas!—that short period of our lives.

For the coach, the practical problem is how to encourage the athlete to adopt and maintain the role that achievement in the event calls for. In general, the high school coach is more concerned with guiding the athlete toward the needed role, and the college coach is more concerned with maintaining the strength of the role. If the athlete has not already adopted a role in secondary school, when he get to college the college coach is working against bad odds if he tries to impose a role on the youth. Even the most highly gifted athlete who has not had a previous role commitment and drifts out to try a sport is not likely to do well. Early in my coaching career a freshman without previous track experience showed up on the field. He was curious about track because his small private school had had no track program. I had him try the high jump, and he cleared six feet two inches the first day. A few days later, he went over six feet five inches. It looked as if he could be the first seven-footer in the world. But he had no background or role as a jumper. He drifted from one sport to another, and in each case the coach became excited about this remarkable talent. But he never took on any specific sports role. His great potential was never realized.

There have been instances in which a fine athlete has a secondary role that is strong enough to lead him to turn out for two sports at the college level. For example, football players often become good weightmen, jumpers, or sprinters. There have been backs who have jumped twenty-four or twenty-five feet without real training or dedication. If they had assumed the role of long-jumper they would have been internationalists. Every so often, with a bit of luck and some skillful handling, the college coach can bring about a strengthening of the secondary role. To the extent that this role becomes stronger, performance is increased.

As suggested earlier, an athletic role is generally acquired before college and very likely the high school coach is a vital factor in that acquisition. However, it's up to the college coach to reinforce the role that's already been acquired. It won't do to assume that the athlete is completely "hooked" by his role and can therefore be depended upon to carry out automatically all the tasks needed for achievement. The college age is one of great flux. Personality is still somewhat plastic. Influences become numerous and diverse. Pressures on the student tend to be intense. New roles become incipient, as they should, with greater maturity. The coach's own enthusiasm for his sport can be a most highly effective instrument in reinforcing an athlete's role. However, if the enthusiasm is blind and bordering on egocentricity, it will probably be damaging. The athlete can be repelled and start wondering about his own enthusiasm.

In the growth process it's inevitable and benign that the college athlete begin to take on other roles, some of which may be the seeds of lifetime roles. It's important for the coach to recognize this reality. He should not try to destroy those roles that he may feel will weaken his own purposes. Instead, he should stress the compatibility

Mental
Rehearsal

The actual instruction and practice on the athletic field form the core of learning sports skills. But in order for an athlete to achieve a fine performance, his work on the field must be augmented by mental rehearsal off the field.

Some years back a highly successful head football coach came to me with an interesting problem. Off season he ran a lucrative insurance business. His main task was to supervise the efforts of his salesmen. An expert consultant persuaded him that mental rehearsal was vital to a successful sales approach. The agent ought to know as much as possible about his sales prospect, including, of course, his insurance needs. But this was only a starter. The data were to provide the base for mental rehearsals. The agent was to run over in his mind what he was going to say, how the prospect would probably respond, what he would say in turn, etc. The sales meetings emphasized the rehearsal method, and, apparently, the method was well accepted by the agents. Sales greatly increased, and all were convinced that mental rehearsal was responsible. The problem for the coach became—how can this method be used to make football players more effective?

The use of mental rehearsal is far from new. It must surely go back to antiquity. The cavemen probably rehearsed mentally their stratagems for hunting and assuring their survival. The military services have always placed a premium on mental rehearsal. For example, the young naval officer standing watch on the bridge of a ship has long been taught to visualize potential emergencies such as a torpedo off the starboard bow, and to rehearse mentally the actions to be taken. Such a procedure would seem bound to pay off in quicker and surer action during an emergency.

I feel confident that almost any athlete who has top-level achievement will testify that he does think about his event off the field. Some of this thinking may not be strictly mental rehearsal. Much of it may be concerned with the fear of not doing well or with fantasies of great performance. If we accept as a working hypothesis that successful athletes give their events considerable off-the-field attention, then some interesting questions arise. To what extent can the athlete's thinking or mental concern with his event be directed toward useful mental rehearsal? What form should this direction take? What is the influence of motivation? What of the nature of the on-the-field input? What interferes with mental rehearsal? What are the roles of the unconscious? Very likely a useful group of questions, but tough ones. At this point it seems best to amplify the questions a bit and anticipate future research findings.

Direction / How successful can efforts be to induce mental rehearsal? In the case of the insurance company, the salesmen agreed that direct efforts to produce mental rehearsal do work. If they do indeed work in a selling effort, it seems possible that direct efforts would work in other areas, including athletics. At present, I don't think we have a formula to offer the coach. Supposedly such an effort would involve group meetings and individual conferences. Some sports psychologists might find it interesting to work with coaches on the feasibility and effects of attempts to encourage and realize mental rehearsal.

Motivation / The problem of mental rehearsal has to tie in with the subject of motivation. The highly motivated athlete is bound to spend a lot of time thinking about his event. This time may be so great that even a small percentage of it given over to mental rehearsal might produce favorable results. In contrast, the poorly motivated athlete probably spends very little time thinking about his event. In his case it hardly seems worthwhile to talk about mental rehearsal until his motivation can be increased.

Input / The most sophisticated computer in the world can't do much without proper input. If the athlete is to profit from mental rehearsal away from the field, his input on the field has to be good. This means that the coaching on the field has to present skills vividly and clearly. The images taken away from the field by the athlete must be as bright as possible. It's difficult to rehearse a hazy script. Needless to say, coaching instruction on the field must be correct from the technical standpoint. If an athlete mentally rehearses a technique that is wrong, he will simply solidify error.

Interference / For most athletes it seems likely that interference with mental rehearsal comes from the pressures of other problems. These pressures compete for the use of both the conscious and unconscious processes.

The observant coach who brought up the topic of mental rehearsal felt that the learning ability of his players declined sharply each year during the early part of November. It was interesting that this perceived drop in learning efficiency coincided with midterm examinations. His university was a high-powered academic one that showed no favor to athletes. The exam period was a grim time and the athletes recognized that both their academic survival and careers were on the line. It's probable that the intense and urgent pressures created by the examinations siphoned off much of the time and energy of the mental processes that otherwise might have been given to the sport.

The athlete does not live in a vacuum. Like the rest of us, in the normal course of living he's bound to have personal problems that clamor for conscious and unconscious attention. The interference with mental rehearsal, however, probably becomes very strong only when a personal problem is almost overwhelming. What can the coach do? His ability to relate to the athlete as a human will be important. To the extent that he can, the coach ought to make himself and his staff available to the athletes. Coaches cannot often produce solutions to personal problems; sometimes they cannot even ease the problems. But as a first step they should at least be approachable.

Unconscious / The process of the unconscious is mysterious, fascinating, and possibly most helpful. From a strictly scientific viewpoint it's difficult to say much about it. But we know it exists. In its thinking process the unconscious does not pay much attention to the formal rules of logic. It takes leaps and bounds in any and all directions. It seems that we cannot have mental rehearsal in any formal sense, but it does seem possible that we can have learning, especially in the form of insights.

The great achievers in science have been so absorbed in their subjects that the subjects have dominated both their conscious and unconscious thinking. By definition unconscious thinking is an underground process. A powerful and almost all-consuming interest in a topic will both activate the unconscious and arm it with data. There is the suspicion that the unconscious can attack a problem relentlessly and constantly, even though the approach is not in the traditional manner. After the conscious has been working on a problem, it may yield an insight to the unconscious, though we don't know by what process. I suppose one of the most famous incidents in which the unconscious produced an insight was that of Archimedes proclaiming "Eureka" in the bathtub. Many great scientists have testified to their debt to unconscious thinking, but in general they seem to resent the part played by the unconscious. They prefer to attribute their accomplishments to the thinking process operating straightaway in a rational manner. Herman von Helmholtz, who made brilliant contributions in the fields of physics, anatomy, and physiology, acknowledged his debt to the unconscious but said, "Those fields of work have become more agreeable to me in which one need not depend on lucky accidents and happy thoughts."

On the field / We've been concerned about mental rehearsal off the field and its importance in bringing about better performance. We ought also to give some attention to on-the-field mental rehearsal. This rehearsal should take place constantly both in practice sessions and in competition. The football player will benefit in both scrimmages and games if he tries to visualize the potential moves of the opposition and mentally rehearse what he will do in reaction to them. The high-jumper will gain by a mental review of what he is going to do on his next jump, whether in practice or competition. The more vivid and concentrated his thoughts, the better. At its most effective, mental

Errors of Anticipation

The ability to anticipate is probably an important biological legacy. Anticipatory reactions may be essential to the survival of infrahumans and are no doubt important and perhaps vital for humans. But we have the curious puzzle that in motor learning, including the acquisition of sports skills, anticipation is the source of nearly all errors, especially those which are resistant to correction. We are drawn to the goal, and along the way our eagerness to arrive makes us neglect intermediate and necessary steps.

The basic task of a coach who teaches the skill events is to change the athlete's performance pattern from one that interferes with progress to one that furthers progress. As the coach carries out his task, he sees the same errors popping up all the time. And nearly all of these errors are rooted in anticipation. The golf instructor, day in and day out, gives the familiar advice, "Keep your head down." But most of us duffers just won't do it consistently. Before the club head makes contact with the ball we look up to admire the ball's flight. But there is little to admire when it bounces and dribbles into the woods. In football it has always been a matter of some curiosity to me that most players cannot kick a football. They can neither punt nor placekick. Teams have to use specialists for kicking, and they are usually small people who would not otherwise be considered for the squad. A professional football roster includes men of extraordinary size, strength, and coordination. If some of these powerhouses could truly learn kicking skills, kicks up to one hundred yards would be likely. But it probably won't happen. Players live by the anticipation of their opponent's moves. They would have a tough psychological task in adjusting to the lack of anticipation that kicking demands.

It is an oddity that in the sports where a great premium is placed on anticipation, anticipation causes the errors. Tennis is a good example. The tennis player lives by anticipation and errs by it. He's got to anticipate where his opponent is likely to hit the ball, and he has to figure out where his opponent is going to be when the ball is returned. But, of course, every teaching pro knows that anticipation interferes with shot making. The hacker tends to have his feet in line parallel to the net. The expert, whenever he has time, places his feet in a line perpendicular to the net for both forehand and backhand. Placing of a shot is important to winning, but the hacker's anticipation of where he is going to hit the ball interferes with a good stroke. The fine player has trained himself to watch the ball until it makes contact with the strings of the racquet. The beginner looks away to see where he is going to hit the ball.

In big league baseball the great hitters have always been remarkable athletes. They surely have superb neuromuscular systems along with good eyesight. Like a fine tennis player, the hitter has to anticipate. He has to anticipate what the pitcher is likely to do, and he may have to figure out the probable moves of the baserunners and the fielders. At the same time, he cannot let anticipation interfere with his concentration on a fast-moving pitch. The ability to keep an eye on the ball almost until it reaches the bat may be what separates the great hitters from the others. The amazing Ted Williams, the last .400 batter in the majors, constantly emphasized the importance of following the ball right to the bat. He is reported to have said that no one can actually see the ball make contact with the bat because he himself had only seen it twice.

Among the various sports skills some of the clearest examples of anticipation adversely affecting performance are seen in the field events. In these events practically all tenacious errors involve anticipation. If an experienced and capable coach kept a log, he'd find out that in his daily practices correcting such errors occupied just about all of his time. Let's consider the long jump. Though the event is simple in nature, very few athletes carry it out well. Their big error is always failure to get enough height. It's no doubt true that no jumper has ever gotten too much height. Great speed is obviously essential to world-class performance. But there have been jumpers who could not make their college teams as sprinters who have done better than twenty-five feet.

When the long-jumper leaves the ground, he is for all practical purposes a projectile. His body has to obey the physical laws governing all projectiles. Once clear of the board the path of his center of gravity is completely set. All that he can do in the air is prepare himself to make the most of the distance covered by his center of gravity. The basic coaching job is to make the jumper concentrate on height. Sounds like an easy coaching task, but it isn't. The psychological pull toward the goal is powerful. For the long-jumper the goal is distance in the pit, and in his struggle to reach the goal directly he slights the height that is needed for distance.

The high jump is similar. Almost any able-bodied youngster would be able to high-jump quite well if he were able to reduce the error of anticipation. The high jump is really a simple event, but most candidates are defeated by anticipation. Stripped to the essentials, performance in the high jump depends upon only two factors—the height to which the body's center of gravity can be driven and the efficiency with which the crossbar can be cleared. The sequence of the two factors is all-important. The lift must come before the clearance is tried. The problem is that the average jumper anticipates the clearance and in this way slights the lift. Lack of height means the clearance efforts become futile.

There are no staggering intellectual concepts in sports techniques. Yet, for example, in the high jump we can often see a bright college student change very little in a career of four years. Intelligence in the academic sense doesn't seem to matter much. Success depends on the ability to overcome anticipation. Anticipation is accompanied by anxiety, which seems to cloud thinking and interfere with execution. If you've coached high-jumpers you may have a tendency to picture them as comic strip characters with balloons over their heads. The balloons indicate the jumper's mental imagery. Before he starts his run toward the bar the balloon shows a clear picture of what he intends to do. He starts his approach and as he nears the bar the balloon in each successive panel shows an increasingly hazy picture. In the last panel, as the jumper is taking off, the balloon is a blank. All imagery has been wiped out. Good execution of form becomes impossible. What remains is only a wild scramble to get over the crossbar.

Sports skills are made up of a series of actions that blend together to make up the complete skill. As indicated earlier, the pole vault can be viewed as consisting of the carry, run, shift, takeoff, rockback, and pull-push. The execution of one act is the base for the correct execution of the next. Hence, if one act in the sequence is carried out poorly, those that follow will also be carried out poorly. In any sequence all of the sub-acts have to be mastered well. But it is much easier to learn the first acts in a series. The reason is simple but significant. Anticipation becomes stronger as the last acts in the series are neared. The first acts are little affected by anticipation, and thus errors can be more readily corrected. Because anticipation becomes stronger, the last acts are usually characterized by tenacious errors.

There seems to be a great deal of similarity between an athlete learning a sports skill and a rat learning a maze. Both are victimized by anticipation. The last moves in the maze are the toughest for the rat. He tends to make the final moves, those closest to the goal, too early. The rat "knows" the right moves, but anticipation interferes with their proper execution. Humans learning a stylus maze do about the same thing.

The shot put, javelin, and discus throws offer clear examples of the effects of anticipation. In these events the great difference between good and poor performers lies in the relative freedom they experience from errors of anticipation. All three events present somewhat similar basic tasks: a build-up of momentum, attainment of a power position from which the big muscles of the body can be used efficiently, and the delivery of the implement. The average thrower never achieves a solid power position, because he anticipates the delivery. The final act is the delivery, and the average athlete is pulled toward that goal.

The result is that the all-important power position is slighted, and there is no base for a good throw.

An athlete's efforts to achieve a new personal best will tend to increase his anxiety and anticipation. This pattern occurs often in the high jump and pole vault especially, because the crossbar is set at a definite height. Hence, the athlete knows that he is trying for a personal best. His anticipation becomes powerful and even his early, corrected errors reappear. His effort will probably be much poorer than those he made at lower heights. But the outlook is good for the future if, along the way, the athlete can lick errors of anticipation. And he can likely go on to perform better. Bob Richards, a truly great athlete, was the second man in the world to clear fifteen feet in the pole vault. He told me that even after he knew that he was capable of making the height, it took him some two hundred vaults before he finally did it. Errors of anticipation got in his way for a time, but he was destined to beat them. Of course, afterward he did better than fifteen feet almost every time he vaulted.

Since I mentioned the second pole vaulter ever to clear fifteen feet, I feel rather obligated to mention the first—the great "Dutch" Warmerdam. In a way I'd rather not because I never understood how he did it. I have never seen a cooler athlete or one less victimized by anticipation. My first clue that he was unflappable came on an occasion when we were both members of an American team competing abroad. One of our meets was held in a soccer stadium in Glasgow before an enormous crowd. No track meet had ever been held in that stadium. There wasn't even a track, much less any facilities for the field events. Everything—the lanes, the hurdles, the landing pits—had to be contrived at the last moment. It was a handicap meet with the local athletes rather favored, the handicaps being a bit unrealistic. One of our teammates held the world record in the high jump. He could have gotten a tie for third in his event—that is, if he had cleared eight feet six inches! With the exception of Warmerdam all of us were upset and griping about the sorry conditions. Warmerdam never changed his expression, though he had the worst deal of all. His task was to run diagonally across a soccer field through a puddle or two, make his pole-plant in a hole that had just been shoveled out, and land in a small mound of sand. Despite all the adversity, though, Warmerdam held his form completely and gave a world-class performance. I shouldn't have been surprised when two years later he became the first fifteen-footer. He was nearing sixteen feet with the old bamboo pole and surely would have made it except that he entered the military service during World War II and was forced to give up his training. I think he would have held form even if he were vaulting at twenty feet.

The extraordinary case of Warmerdam represents an extreme end of a spectrum. The coach can realistically expect to deal with athletes who are constantly plagued by errors of anticipation, errors that seem completely resistant to correction. What can the coach do? Well, coaching is, after all, an art. An artist undergoes training in his craft, but he cannot be told how to create a masterpiece. Nevertheless, a few coaching suggestions might be helpful.

1. When anticipation is the heart of the learning problem, as it usually is, it must be recognized as such. If an athlete is not performing well, many coaches try one gimmick after another without really coming to grips with the problem. It doesn't do to deal in irrelevancies just to have something to say. Coaching approaches will and should vary with the ingenuity of the coach, but he ought to know what he's dealing with. There are many roads to Rome, but it's nice to know where Rome is.

2. Put the burden on the athlete as much as possible. After all, it's his event. Let him do some thinking. Make his intelligence an important force. After a candidate for the high jump has had some preliminary orientation, he can be asked a simple question like "What makes a jumper go high?" Or a discus thrower can be asked, "What makes a discus travel far?" Such questions will not produce results magically, but they will tend to plant seeds of thought. The athlete may at least reach an understanding of what must be done. If he does, there is a better chance that effective ideas will creep into his form.

3. In line with the previous point, a sometimes highly effective procedure is to make the athlete a kind of "assistant coach" within a limited area. To make matters concrete, let's get back to our example of the high-jumper. Suppose that a track coach has, as he surely will, a varsity high-jumper who suffers from the typical anticipatory error of inadequate takeoff. A good procedure might be to put the athlete partly in charge of a beginner with instructions somewhat as follows: "He doesn't seem to understand that the key to good jumping is a good lift. He keeps trying to scramble over the bar before he really jumps. Try to help him." Both the student coach and the beginner are likely to benefit. Through the process of active coaching the jumper's attention is increasingly drawn to the really critical act of the event.

4. It's already been suggested that in the sequence of acts that compose a motor skill the acts toward the end of the series are the most disturbed by anticipation. Of course, the division of an event's flow of motion into discrete actions is somewhat artificial and sometimes arbitrary. Even so, it turns out to be a useful procedure. For practical purposes we can identify the various acts in a sequence. The final acts in any series are the ones most adversely affected by anticipation. Most difficulty in learning an event involves acts that take place just before the final act. The execution of these acts determines whether the carrying out of the final act is going to be relatively easy or impossible. To oversimplify a bit, there is an act or several acts

that occur just prior to the final one that are vital in setting up the effectiveness of performance. To go back to our now-familiar example of the high jump, we obviously want an efficient clearance, but we can't have it without a good takeoff. Because of the time relationship it is most difficult for the athlete to associate any act other than the final one with the quality of his performance. Getting the athlete to associate the critical act with effective performance is a tough coaching job. But the coach can still harp away at the critical act. After all, frequency can have an influence in bringing about a correct response.

5. One of the promising ways to reduce errors of anticipation and anxiety is to try to get the athlete to gain more conscious control of his actions. An approach that I have found useful is as follows. The athlete, let's say a vaulter, is asked to participate in a kind of experiment. It is suggested that we carry out a series of tries in which the only goal is to make a report. The vaulter is told that in this series of vaults the criterion of success will be entirely different from the usual one of height. "The measure of success," I tell him, "will be the clarity of your report, and nothing else matters. If you clear the bar by a foot and can't tell me what you did, it's a poor vault. If you miss by a mile but can tell me what went on, it's a good vault."

After the first try the athlete may report, "Coach, I don't remember a thing from the time I took off until I landed in the pit." A report such as this may at first seem dismal, but it has optimistic overtones. For one thing, it suggests that the report method might be very appropriate for the athlete. As the vaulter refines his method of reporting with each successive vault, his reports are likely to become clearer and his athletic form better. Like other psychological approaches this one can't be guaranteed to be surefire. Yet empirically it seems to have a demonstrated value. On the theoretical side, the method seems psychologically sound. It is easy to see that if the athlete is temporarily released from the task of succeeding—the task that traditionally pleases the coach—he is then relieved of a certain amount of anxiety and is therefore freer to give more attention to technique. He is more apt to concentrate on the significant acts of the series. Also, the analysts have made the point that learning is seldom brought about if unconscious factors are dominant. Neurotic behavior is based on unconscious dynamics, and one of the hallmarks of neurotic behavior is that it is not amenable to the so-called normal laws of learning.

This method—making the athlete report—should not be only a one-time affair. A certain amount of anticipation is always present, and potential errors are ready to pop up—even in the highly advanced athlete. If the method of report can be considered a treatment, the beginner should get a great deal of it. The expert can use a small dose when he lapses into a slump.

Before we leave the area of anticipatory errors, I think we have to make a modifying point. Anticipation does cause most motor errors, but a certain amount of anticipation is needed, especially at the very top levels of performance. There has to be a fine balance between giving each act its due concentration and getting ready for the next one. For example, in fiberglass vaulting the task is to get maximum energy into the pole and then make the best use of this energy in getting height over the crossbar. For top performance there has to be an almost instantaneous switch in perception or attention—and at precisely the right moment. The vaulter has to concentrate fully on his takeoff. But once he is even less than a thousandth of an inch clear of the ground, he can put no more energy into the pole. His attention then has to move quickly to his body position on the pole. In brief, we have two acts in the sequence that are a tiny fraction of a second apart. There is no time to ponder between these acts. Hence, there has to be some anticipation of the second act when the first is taking place. Though such anticipation is needed, interference has to be kept to a minimum. The timing is delicate and usually only attained by top performers.

In the skill events, most coaching and learning time will be spent in overcoming errors of anticipation. The process is bound to be frustrating and even discouraging at times. But these errors should not be regarded as an eternal curse. Rather, they should be viewed as a challenge; licking them is a big part of the fun of the game. Psychologically, errors of anticipation are a bright spot. They indicate both a desire to do well and a relative freedom from fear of success. More about that later.

Psychological Limits

There cannot be the slightest doubt about the existence of psychological barriers to achievement in sports. Obviously, there have to be physical limits to what can be done, but it may be that no athlete has ever reached his absolute physical potential. The psychological limit comes first.

A pattern familiar to experienced coaches is that in which the athlete improves rapidly and then levels off. He reaches a kind of plateau similar to that seen in laboratory learning experiments. It often appears at a high level of performance. The athlete may already be a scorer in championship competition and appear ready to be next year's winner. All at once his progress stops, even though he continues to work hard—sometimes apparently even harder than before. It would seem natural enough to conclude that he's reached his physical potential. But a close look at the workout shows this isn't so. Routine errors that once could be corrected quickly now become tenacious. If an error is eliminated through intensive coaching, another error pops up to take its place. The errors are induced by the need not to go on to a higher level of achievement. The athlete has not reached a physical limit, but he has reached a level of mental comfort.

In my own coaching I have dealt with the above pattern a number of times. I was never too successful in doing much about it even though I felt that something could have and should have been done. I recall one youngster who had no athletic experience in secondary school but had a fantastic rise in college. He improved rapidly until he was placing in championship meets. He leveled off during an Olympic year. Even though he had stopped improving, he still had a reasonably good chance of making the U.S. Olympic team. He told me that he couldn't afford to train for the team or even make the trip abroad because he had to earn money for next year's tuition. His father was a millionaire who picked up the tuition bill with neither discomfort nor displeasure. But the youngster was not to be faulted. He had done very well and had contributed valuable points to team victories. It was just that he wouldn't be comfortable as an Olympian. I don't think the process was at all conscious. If the athlete were confronted by this analysis he would be startled.

The pattern of psychological limits can be observed in sports activities, but the same pattern exists in other areas of life. An office employee, for example, might have been carrying out work faithfully, loyally, efficiently, and comfortably for many years. His employers, taking into account his fine service, want to do something for him. The reward may be elevation to office manager. If he can, he will avoid the promotion. But if it is thrust on him and there is no escape, he may have had his last well day. From then on he may suffer from headaches and other symptoms of tension arising from the "reward." His level of comfort has been passed.

Coaches are often asked to explain the record explosion of recent years, because they are the experts. But I think those closest to athletics are the most baffled. In general, a reasonable stock answer seems to be that the great performances of today are attributable to new training methods and superior facilities. New methods such as repetition training, interval training, and weight training really are not all that new. All of them have been tried over the years by a number of outstanding athletes, though more athletes are now using these methods. Athletic facilities are greatly improved, but today's greats could perform on the old facilities and still break records. The psychological factors have to be the most important of all.

During the early fifties three "magic" marks of track and field were passed. Roger Bannister ran a sub–four-minute mile. Parry O'Brien put the shot better than sixty feet. Charles Dumas jumped higher than seven feet.

Some physiologists and other experts had calculated that a four-minute mile was impossible. From the physical standpoint man could not do it, they claimed. But if it could be done, Bannister seemed to be the ideal prospect. He was gifted athletically, highly intelligent, scientifically oriented, and thoroughly dedicated. When he made his actual try, he was paced by the finest milers in Great Britain. At the finish, Bannister was completely exhausted. It appeared as if he had expended every ounce of his energy and done so in an efficient and scientific way. Yet, a little while later, Landy ran 3:58. Look at the present situation. There have been many hundreds of sub–four-minute miles. In some races even the last-place finisher has done better than four minutes. And many schoolboys have bettered four minutes.

The records in the shot put have been puzzling. In the early thirties the world record was exchanged by several athletes at the fifty-two-feet-plus level. At the Olympic Games of 1932 the shot put was won by Leo Sexton with a new record of fifty-two feet six inches. An abrupt rise in the record came two years later when Jack Torrance, a massive giant of 280 pounds, with speed and agility enough to excel in both football and basketball, went to work on the record. He moved it up to more than fifty-five feet. Later that year he got off the then-incredible put of fifty-seven feet one inch. It was pronounced a perfect record, along with Bill Carr's 46.2 for the 400 meters.

Time went by, and Torrance's record wasn't even approached. National championships were won at fifty-one and fifty-two feet. Torrance himself failed to make fifty-one feet in the 1936 Olympic Games. It did seem that the record might be "perfect" as the experts thought. Many powerful men tried for it and failed. However, some fourteen years after the record was set, it was broken by Chuck Fonville of Michigan. Then Jim Fuchs of Yale took charge and broke the record routinely. Fuchs at 228 pounds was an absolute powerhouse. He could do more than fifty one-arm push-ups and run the hundred yards in 9.7 seconds. He was extremely bright and developed a technique that motion pictures show to be almost flawless. Also, he was a fierce competitor who had the thought that given one more put, he could beat anybody on earth. He usually did. If I were coaching today and looking for someone to break the present world record, I would look for an athlete with Fuchs's qualifications. Why, then, was his best a dozen feet short of today's record?

The shot put of sixty feet had to await Parry O'Brien. Parry had great qualifications in every way. He was big, strong, fast, and agile. Further, he had the advantage of weight training, which had come into widespread use. He was an ingenious technician and invented the form that still bears his name. Parry's extraordinary physical qualifications were equaled by his mental ones. It's hard to imagine a person with more drive and dedication. He worked out three times a day, thought about his event when not working out, and then played tapes at bedtime to make sure that his sleeping hours weren't wasted. What happened to him? He won the Olympic title in 1952. He went on to break the world record over and over again, and in 1956 he broke his own Olympic record by almost four feet. He continued to improve, but by 1960, though he put some two feet past his Olympic record, he had to settle for the silver medal. By the 1964 Games Parry had improved some more, but this time there was no medal. The field was passing him by.

High school boys have bettered sixty feet, and at the present writing there are more than half a dozen shot-putters who have beaten seventy feet. I've emphasized Parry O'Brien's astonishing characteristics because they make the obliteration of his marks difficult to understand. We have a real puzzle. The solution has to be psychological. How was he surpassed by athletes with lesser physical qualifications? Surely none of the many who have put farther matched him in dedication or intensity. In fact, some of them have seemed rather casual in their approaches.

The great Bill Carr was never beaten in a race, either in prep school or college. In 1932 Carr won the Olympic 400 meters in a time of 46.2, which was considered one of the two "perfect" records in track and field. His running career was ended by an injury he received in what appeared to be an odd automobile accident. Of course, the assault on the perfect record began. Some years ago Carr's old coach said to me, "More than a hundred runners have bettered Bill's time. But if you had all of them at their best, including Bill, and lined them up for a race, Bill would not come in last."

The barrier of seven feet which so long defied high-jumpers is passed just about every day. The world record, at this writing, is seven feet, eight and one-half inches. We've reached the point where a mere seven-footer is not a serious candidate for a major meet. This year more than twenty-eight American jumpers have surpassed seven feet.

The fantastic Jesse Owens's best time for the hundred yards was 9.4 seconds. It would be difficult to list all of the sprinters who have beaten Jesse's best time. The present world record is 9.0, and many sprinters have turned in 9.1 performances. Suppose we picture Owens at his best, running against a field of 9.1 sprinters. They would, according to the numbers, have a blanket finish with Jesse picking up dust about ten feet behind them. Those of us who have seen Owens run would have great difficulty accepting such a picture.

The pattern we've been talking about seems to be mysterious. As new standards of performance they tend to create a tolerance of or a comfort with greater achievement. Some sort of inhibition seems to be reduced, and athletes, including the average ones, are freer to perform better. The greats of the past seemed to be all-out and without inhibitions. But perhaps they weren't.

The ability of a new generation to adjust to almost anything in the environment is astonishing. When the atomic bomb was dropped on Hiroshima, my ship was in the Philippines. Our news report was scanty, but we sat in the wardroom trying to figure out what it was all about. One fellow officer was a physicist and came up with what turned out to be a pretty good explanation of things. I sat and brooded over the new atomic age. My special concern was with the mental health of children who would have to grow up under the great atomic menace. I'm still worrying, but the kids don't seem all that bothered. When I was a youngster, if a television set had appeared in the living room it would have had to be attributed to witchcraft. Today, little tots waddle across the room and tune in their favorite programs. The computer still is to me an incredible development, and I'm still thrown off balance by it. But students simply go ahead and use it as a device that's available to them. Acceptance of the standards of the time!

I think that the world-record holder tends to have special psychological problems. He is not just moving along with the advancing standards of his day. He is venturing ahead of them. He is pioneering. Because he is leaving a level of mental comfort, he may have to pay a toll—perhaps even a safeguard against further advance. John Thomas broke the world high-jump record with a leap of seven feet three and three-quarters inches. Afterwards he injured his foot by catching it in an elevator. Valery Brumel added two inches to Thomas's record. But Brumel suffered a motorcycle accident in which the bones of his takeoff leg were smashed beyond surgical repair. I happened to know both athletes rather well. I can't think of two better adjusted young men. But maybe the toll simply has to be exacted when you go ahead of your time.

In running we've had two cases of startling world-record performers in Jim Ryun and Ron Clarke. Ryun was an absolute prodigy, running the mile in under four minutes while still in high school. He went on to break world records in the half-mile, 1,500 meters, and mile. He was a clear favorite to win the 1,500 meters at the 1968 Olympics in Mexico City. He ended up second, but it did seem he would have won had it not been for the altitude of Mexico

City and an illness he had before the Games. Later Ryun began to run some disappointing races and even began to drop out of some. However, he seemed to be in excellent physical shape for the 1972 Games at Munich. One coach reported that Ryun had run two practice half-miles of 1:51 that were practically back to back. This remarkable practice performance indicated extraordinary physical readiness. But Ryun never reached the finals. In a preliminary heat he came into contact with another runner and fell. Later on, as a member of the professional circuit, he was constantly beaten in plus-four-minute miles. Also, the dropout pattern reappeared. Everywhere one heard the question: "What's wrong with Ryun?" Maybe nothing, except perhaps he paid the price for his pioneering.

Ron Clarke of Australia was probably just as remarkable as Ryun. Over a period of time he set and reset world records in the distance runs. His records seemed unbelievable. Yet, as far ahead of the field as he was on a time basis, he always had trouble with major opponents and was almost always defeated in important international competition. There is the suggestion that Clarke's pioneering took its toll.

It would seem foolish to argue about whether psychological limitations exist. They surely do, and the task is to understand more about them. In our efforts we are likely to come up with notions that will appear farfetched to the "practical" coach. But, at one time, Freud's ideas seemed absurd too. And the idea that the earth is round instead of flat once seemed an affront to common sense.

My approach to psychological limitation in sports achievement relies heavily on the concept of inhibition. Of course, inhibition cannot be directly perceived. It has to be inferred. And in the subtle area in which we are working, inferences are difficult to make. The coach might quickly accept the notion of inhibition in the cases of many of his athletes. He may even volunteer the judgment that they are not approaching their potential. But he will cite examples where athletes completely exhaust themselves every day in practice and in the competitions. Their efforts seem all-out and free of inhibitions. But could it be that their exhaustion is partly attributable to their inhibition?

The degree of inhibition, I feel, is largely determined unconsciously by a frame of reference. The frame of reference amounts to what other people are doing at a given time. For example, a generation ago, the good discus thrower was a 160-footer competing against the top throwers who were doing better than 170 feet. At the present time, a good discus thrower is a 190-footer who competes against the 200–plus throwers. So it goes with all of the other sports events. The mass moves along just behind the world-record holders. The records of yesteryear's greats are not just beaten by new greats; they are trampled upon by multitudes.

In our speculation and research efforts we tend to ignore the nonquantitative sports like football, boxing, basketball, and hockey. That's because in these sports only the most primitive measurement exists. If one team or individual defeats another, about all we can say is that at a given moment A was greater than B. If by some magic method we could attach a valid number to a team or individual performance, we would surely find that today's players are better than those of yesterday. I think we might be pretty close to assessment of performance if we extrapolate from the quantitative sports. Then we would have to say that our present athletes in the nonquantitative sports, such as boxing, are better than yesterday's heroes—although this would upset the barroom debaters.

Having talked about psychological limitations produced by inhibition, I can't say any specific prescriptions have yet emerged. The reduction of the inhibitions seems largely a result of our times. The inexorable march of progress continues, and with this march frames of reference change. Inhibitions are reduced and performances improve. I don't know if quick efforts to reduce individual inhibitions are useful or indicated. Hypnosis has been tried, but it doesn't seem to work. Other methods may possibly be successful.

There are differences between performance in team sports and individual sports. From the psychological standpoint the main difference, though there are others, centers around the freedom to express aggression. The team player is freer. Psychologically, it's easier to take the position of "Come on gang. Let's get them." "I've got to get them" is more difficult. A rifleman who cannot fire alone may be able to fire as a member of a squad.

In brief, I have been suggesting that the inhibition that restricts expression of aggression becomes less restrictive in a team sport. However, the situation may be rapidly changing at the top level of some sports, especially professional football. Television features individual players, thus putting a greater premium on expressing individual aggression.

Observation

Perception is a vital coaching need. Without an accurate and clear perception of what the athlete is doing, effective coaching cannot take place.

Suppose we see a vault being made. The casual spectator sees little more than that the vaulter runs, gets off the ground, and either clears the crossbar or knocks it off. The beginning coach will see more. He will probably perceive the parts of the vault and even be able to assess how well some of them were carried out. The expert coach will be able to see nearly all of the parts with great clarity. Particularly, he will perceive the critical points of the vault that make for success or failure. His perception may be so vivid that he can rerun the vault in his mind like a motion picture. To say that the expert has a "sharp eye" is only a figurative expression. The eyes are only a starting point.

Perception takes place in the brain. The specialized sense organs can only receive appropriate stimulation and transmit nervous impulses to the brain. Vision is a highly complicated process. Even in the case of the "sharp eye" the retina is only stimulated by a focused pattern of light waves. The impulses on the retina have to be carried by relays to the visual center of the brain. The visual center has the further complexity of integrating reports emanating from two eyes. Interestingly, while the eyes are in front, the center of vision is in the back of the head.

We are bombarded by raw sensations, and the brain has to interpret these sensations to bring about perceptions. At birth we start from scratch. There are only sensations. Perception is a matter of learning. The topic of perception has been a serious problem for philosophers throughout the ages and apparently still is. The relationship between sensation and perception was an important legacy to psychologists when they broke with philosophy. The early experimental psychologists were highly occupied with the problem. Not all aspects of the sensation-perception relationship have been solved, but we do know that learning is critical to our perceptions.

Not to get into an involved philosophical problem, I think we have to take it for granted that through common biography we share, at least roughly, some perceptions with our fellows. When we perceive tables and chairs we have confidence that others are also perceiving tables and chairs. However, the furniture maker or dealer will have a sharper perception of these objects than the rest of us. We can perceive snow, but not in the way the Eskimo does. For him snow is a critical day-to-day reality. He has no word for snow as such. Instead, he has various words to designate snow under different conditions—such as falling snow, drifting snow, and caked snow.

Sherlock Holmes trained himself to perceive clues that had no meaning for the perplexed Doctor Watson. To Holmes the perceptions were "elementary" because of his background. When we hear a strange foreign language we are dealing with almost pure auditory sensation. There is little or no perception. We simply lack the appropriate background. The skilled internist can listen to a heartbeat and perceive what we can't perceive. He has the necessary background.

A youngster who is intensively interested in automobiles can usually identify the make, year, and model of any car that he sees. His perception is quick. He can even identify a car that passes in a fraction of a second. If you ask him how he does it, he'll be surprised and mention such "obvious" features as door handles, grid, etc. His interest brought about his own informal training in perception. The formal training used by the armed services has shown how much perception can be sharpened. The great majority of trainees could learn to identify an aircraft in a fraction of a second.

Once there are stimuli, perception becomes a function of the central nervous system. It's an internal process with the brain doing the work. However, the brain can't do the job of interpretation unless it has been previously prepared, or "programmed." There has to be a structure or background that permits sensations to be put in order so that perceptions can be formed. This ability, resulting from training and interest, has been termed "apperception background." The phrase seems useful.

The physician who has inadequate training or a declining interest in his profession cannot make an accurate diagnosis. His prescription is not likely to be helpful. It could in fact be injurious. So it is with the athletic coach who lacks training and interest. He can't have a clear perception of what the athlete is doing. He can't say anything useful, and the chances are he'll say something irrelevant or harmful to performance.

The high school coach often has an especially difficult task in building up the needed apperception backgrounds. Because of staffing restrictions and austerity conditions he may be assigned to coach sports in which he has little or no background. This is likely because school systems want mileage from a coach. They want him to be a "man for all seasons." They want him to coach something in the fall, something in the winter, and something in the spring. Fortunately for the coach, the schools are closed in the summer.

As suggested, the high school coach is likely to be thrust into situations that are unfamiliar to him. The coach who has some background in basketball and feels comfortable there may, come spring, find that he is the baseball or the track coach. He will be confronted by youngsters who have more knowledge and background than he has. For example, if he takes over track and field and has on the squad a six-foot jumper, a twelve-foot vaulter, and a fifty-foot shot-putter, he is going to be dealing with young athletes who have given their events a lot of energy and attention. They are not likely to be especially knowledgeable, but they will have some sort of orientation, including a smattering of the jargon of their events. The coach has a tricky task. At the outset the athletes assume that the coach knows something about the events or he wouldn't be the coach. Also, the enthusiastic athlete is so egocentric about his own event that he assumes other people share his enthusiasm and even some of his knowledge. Thus, at least at first, the reception given the new coach may not be too bad. He can, however, hurt himself by saying too many of the wrong things. The athletes tend to consider the new coach competent until the coach himself disproves it.

When a coach is assigned to an unfamiliar sport, he has very little apperception background. How then should he proceed? First, he should be cautious about saying too much in areas where he is not qualified. Second, he can utilize general principles that may carry over from a sport that is familiar to him. There are some principles that carry over from sport to sport. For example, nearly all athletic performance requires good balance. The topic of balance isn't simple, however, since you can have balance under static conditions and under various conditions of movement. A capable football coach knows the importance of balance and has the background to perceive it. He knows that if a lineman is off balance he can't be effective in either making a block or resisting one. Even if the coach knows nothing about the shot put, for example, he can make a useful contribution if he just emphasizes the athlete's need for maintaining his balance.

As suggested, a coach who is experienced in one sport does not enter another completely cold. There should be enough transfer to permit him to make a contribution. Yet the use of transfer can be regarded as merely a start, a chance for the coach to get his foot in the door. After that, the coach must immerse himself in his new sport. Only in this way can he acquire the apperception background needed for observation. If a coach does have to handle several different sports, he can only do his best with the time and energy available to him. It's unrealistic to aspire to be a top observer in all sports. The best observers are going to be specialists.

A coach establishes the base for his career very early in the game. It's then that he can and should put energy into training himself to observe. The older he gets, the more difficult it will be for him to acquire an apperception background. The young coach can get away with asking naive questions and making mistakes. The more "established" coach cannot. The coach who has not learned his events early in his career is destined to have some uncomfortable moments, and to do some poor coaching. Unfortunately, there are many examples of coaches who, through happenstance or recruiting, have become nationally prominent. Let's say one such coach has on his team a group of talented vaulters. He dare not try to coach them for fear of saying something dumb that would leave the athletes aghast. He has to bluff, which makes for a long and tiring day for him.

To summarize, a coach can be effective only if he is a good observer of his sport. He should build up an apperception background in the areas in which he coaches. This takes interest, energy, and effort. Training in observation should come about as early as possible in the coach's career.

Those Who Cannot Compete

The differences among athletes in their ability to perform when the chips are down present a fascinating and challenging problem. Under stress of competition some athletes rise to unexpected heights, while others fall apart. The pattern is stable and has probably always existed. Many years ago, the famous Irish weight throwers made frequent use of the phrase "morning glory." They were referring to the athletes who could do well in the morning practice and then, like the morning glory, fade and fold in the afternoon's competition.

The pattern of competitive ability is easily illustrated. Suppose, for example, two high-jumpers clear six feet, six inches in practice. In the actual competition the "good" competitor may approach seven feet, while the "poor" competitor may have trouble with six feet. Several days later in practice both will again be clearing the same

Note: I am indebted to the Yale University Press for permission to use or rework certain materials contributed by me to *Psychosocial Problems of College Men*, edited by Bryant M. Wedge, 1955.

height, only to separate again in the next competition. Parry O'Brien was one of the great competitors of all time. Once warmed up for his practice, he made every put as if his life depended on it. Afterward, he would measure his best all-out put and then pick a spot some four feet farther. He said that this was the distance he was going to reach in competition. He always did. In contrast, some shot-putters drop four feet in the meet.

The differential ability to compete probably exists at all levels of physical potential, but the inability to compete when the potential is great is an enormous source of wonder and frustration to the coach. Great physical potential without its expression in public competition is usually known only to the coach. The amount of potential of some noncompetitors can be truly incredible. I personally know of two athletes who broke Olympic records while performing well below their routine practice performances. As far as the general public could surmise, these athletes had done extremely well; after all, they were Olympic champs. An athlete whom I coached placed in three events in a championship competition. His points were most welcome, and as far as other coaches and spectators could make out, he had turned in rather fine performances. However, I, and perhaps he, knew that if he had been able to overcome serious psychological obstacles he would have broken the records in all three events.

In the team sports it's much more difficult to spot the poor competitor. The football player who barely misses a block, tackle, or pass looks as if he might do well the next time. But the same "bad breaks" continue to occur. In the quantitative sports the inability to compete should be easy to see. Yet it is not easily credited by the coach. He can't believe what he's perceived. Surely, he thinks, the non-competitor will straighten out and perform in accordance with his abilities. But he doesn't. Because the coach has usually been a good competitor, he is baffled by the poor competitor's behavior. It is difficult for the coach to realize that he may be dealing with a rather permanent pattern.

In my discussions with various coaches I found that the inability to compete was a fairly frequent topic. However, it was regarded as a temporary situation that required just a bit of handling. Also, the pattern was not associated with any constellation of personality traits. Yet, with descriptions of more and more cases, the good and the poor competitors began to exhibit rather different personality portraits. Competitive ability was apparently not an isolated facet of behavior.

The preliminary findings were interesting enough to suggest further exploration. I wanted to see if reports from a broader sample of coaches throughout the nation would validate what we seemed to be finding. A questionnaire was formulated to be sent to selected track coaches. Sixty-five track and field coaches were picked on the basis of the intensity and fullness of their programs. Track seemed a logical sport for two reasons. First, it is highly quantitative. Second, the observational opportunities offered by track and field are exceptional in that the coaching method is largely tutorial and the season is longer than that of most other sports.

An effort was made to keep the questionnaire both short and realistic. The coach was not asked for theoretical views, nor was he asked to make observations that were not readily available to him. Questions were restricted to behavior that a coach could be expected to observe during the normal course of his coaching contact with the athlete.

Each participating coach was mailed two copies of the questionnaire, one to apply to a good competitor and the other to a poor competitor. Directions were as follows:

Good Competitor

By checking the appropriate box, please answer the questions below about the best or one of the best competitors you have ever coached. The man you consider for these questions need not be a present member of the squad. He can be anyone who generally seems or seemed to rise above his practice performances in competition. We won't need his name. If the responses listed for a question are not adequate, please write in the appropriate answer. Use the reverse side if necessary.

Poor Competitor

By checking the appropriate box, please answer the questions below about the worst or one of the worst competitors you have ever coached. The man you consider for these questions need not be a present member of the squad. He can be anyone who generally seems or seemed to blow up or go to pieces in competition, i.e., not able to approach his practice performance. We won't need his name. If the responses listed for a question are not adequate, please write in the appropriate answer. Use the reverse side if necessary.

The questionnaire, along with the results, is shown in the table. It consisted of thirteen behavioral and personality items. Sixty-five sets of questionnaires were mailed. All but three were returned. In all, there were fifty-seven usable questionnaires on the good competitor and sixty on the poor. About half of the coaches wrote personal letters expressing some of their views. However, none of the letters contained theoretical formulations. Some coaches showed a misunderstanding of the effort. Some expressed interest and offered encouragement. A few assured me that I wouldn't find any personality differences between the good and poor competitors. One down-to-earth coach wrote across the questionnaire on the poor competitor: "I think he's nuts."

Subject selection was, of course, determined by the coaches, who were given the option of picking a single good competitor and a single poor competitor. Though coaches were not asked to name the subjects, most of them did name the good competitors. These included many of the all-time greats of track and field. Selection of subjects on a quantitative basis would not have worked out well. The pattern that we were examining represents a disparity between a base performance level, which reflects practice performance and other indications of physical capacity, and competitive performance. Measures of the latter are matters of record, but the base measures are less amenable to direct measurement. The very use of predetermined measurements, even in the absence of formal competition, would tend to create a test atmosphere. Thus, such measurements would likely reflect competitive ability. The poor competitor would be sensitive to even the most informal type of measurement. Case data indicate that his good practice performance can cease abruptly if there is much attention focused on it by either his teammates or his coach.

THE RESULTS

Item 1 is the only one that failed to produce a statistically significant difference. Preliminary findings had indicated that the poor competitor has a tendency to practice at odd hours and in this way avoid the regular workout routine. Too, it was found that the athlete could operate in such a

Coaches' Ratings of Good and Poor Competitors

Item	Responses	Good	Poor
1. What time of the day does he (did he) usually come to practice?	Earlier in the day than most men	11	12
	About the same time as most	43	38
	Later than most	3	6
	Other	0	4
2. Does he work hard in practice?	Lazy—needs to be pushed	1	5
	About average	4	19
	Hard worker	50	32
	Other	2	2
3. When he talks about future performance, is he shooting for	The next meet?	40	23
	Late season?	2	3
	Some eventual performance?	10	28
	Other	5	6
4. After a poor competitive showing, does he blame	Conditions, officials, etc?	2	10
	Himself?	44	38
	Both?	1	10
	Other	10	2
5. Is he considered	A lone wolf?	1	18
	Very friendly?	42	12
	About average?	13	28
	Other	1	2
6. Does he seem to be happy?	Usually in good spirits, has plenty of belly laughs	31	16
	Smiles easily, but seldom laughs heartily	24	29
	Seldom smiles or laughs	1	15
	Other	1	0

Item	Responses	Good	Poor
7. Does he tend to be	The life of the party?	15	9
	About average?	35	25
	Very quiet?	7	21
	Other	0	5
8. Does he make sense in his conversation?	Always rational and coherent	46	15
	About average	10	32
	Conversation sometimes seems strange and hard to follow	1	12
	Other	1	1
9. Does he follow coaching instruction well?	Usually follows instructions well without comment	43	19
	Follows instructions well but often with comment	14	16
	Usually makes out a case for doing something different	0	21
	Other	0	4
10. Does he learn easily?	Learns well	47	13
	An average learner	8	31
	Has great difficulty in learning some things	2	14
	Other	0	2
11. Does he talk easily?	Communication good	48	23
	About average	9	23
	Difficult to talk to	0	13
	Other	0	1
12. Is he popular with his teammates?	Well liked	48	14
	About average	7	30
	Unpopular	1	15
	Other	1	1

Item	Responses	Good	Poor
13. What is his reaction following a good competitive performance?	Likely to make another good performance the following week	51	0
	Likely to make an average performance the following week	4	21
	Likely to fall off badly in the next meet	1	29
	Other	1	1

Note: Distributions of responses on each item for good and poor competitors were compared by means of the chi-square technique. With the exception of Item 1, differences were significant at less than the .01 level of confidence.

---

subtle fashion that often the coach was not aware of the pattern. Classes and labs that didn't exist were often used as excuses. The results show only a slight tendency for the "poors" to be reported as showing less conformity in their practice times. It may be that many institutions are so organized in the use of facilities that there is not enough flexibility for the athlete to practice at odd hours.

Item 2 was included mostly to establish that the poor competitors are committed to the activity—i.e., that their poor performances are not a result of indifference. The good competitors were considered harder workers, but only six subjects, one good and five poor, were called lazy.

Item 3 supports the preliminary finding that the poor competitor shows more interest in some ultimate performance than in an immediate one. In our earlier investigations we had found that some of the poor competitors seemed to have informal timetables calling for achievement after they would actually be finished with competition. The poor competitor can accept the notion of achievement when it does not seem too imminent.

Item 4, the only one to reverse preliminary findings, reports the poor as being somewhat more extrapunitive than the good competitor. This reversal is surprising in view of the very strong tendency shown in our earlier cases for the poor competitor to accept, or almost proclaim, the blame for poor performances. My own experience has been so persuasive, and even overwhelming, that I have to wonder about the questionnaire results. There could be a strong "halo" effect, since it is considered noble for a person to accept the blame for his poor performance.

Items 5 through 8 represent, as do the other items, an attempt to check on an empirical pattern. Yet these items do seem to have the flavor of an "adjustment inventory." The poor competitor would appear to be unhappier, more constricted, and in general more poorly adjusted. He seems to have difficulty in expressing his aggression, and his inability to compete in athletics may be a specific instance of such an overall difficulty. Since there is a strong suggestion that the poor competitor is ambivalent about motivation, there is a theoretical expectation that he will show greater personal conflict.

Item 9, which shows a differential reaction to coaching instruction, may represent the operation of a number of factors. There is reason to expect a negative reaction to authority and adults on the part of the poor competitor. In addition, our preliminary findings had suggested that the poor competitor prefers to structure his workouts in such a way as to preclude real achievement. In other words, a fear could exist that the instructions given by the coach may bring about success. A similar, and equally tentative, view may be taken toward the results of Item 10, which indicate that the poor competitor has greater difficulty in learning. The differential ability to communicate, reported in Item 11, may represent both a difference in attitude toward adults and an inability to express aggression. Item 12 backs up our earlier view that the poor competitor is rather a withdrawn personality.

Item 13, I think, produced some extraordinary results. They are so extreme that it's hard to credit them, but they are completely in line with our own experience. A poor competitor who happens to hit a good performance is really done for a while. The reaction of the poor competitor would surely seem to be outside of the so-called normal laws of learning, especially the "law of effect." A prevalent coaching stereotype seems to be destroyed. The coaching prescription for the poor competitor is indicated by such expressions as: "He'll be all right after he gets a good performance under his belt"; "As soon as he 'tastes a little blood' he'll have a desire to win"; "Nothing breeds success like success," etc. Apparently a taste of "success" does anything but reassure a poor competitor. Whatever the anxieties or other interferences that prevent good performance, they are heightened by the happenstance of success.

I can remember a track and field coach who had a very fine team. All events were well covered except for one. In an early-season meet a runner turned in an excellent performance in the weak event. The coach was jubilant and kept telling me that the squad was now complete. I happened to know the athlete, and he fitted the personality portrait of the poor competitor just about completely. I didn't think the coach ought to live in a fool's paradise, so I mentioned that the athlete's performance was probably his last good one for a while. He rejected this suggestion, calling it "farfetched." He said that he personally held a stopwatch on the run and knew the performance to be genuine. The athlete never again approached his early performance.

SOME FURTHER OBSERVATIONS

The questionnaire sent to the coaches was an attempt to test a number of points that emerged from earlier efforts to investigate competitive ability pretty much on a case basis. Though for practical reasons the questions had to be limited, the results did in general lend striking support to our earlier findings. The responses of the coaches are illuminating in themselves, but I think we would be remiss if we did not discuss some of the early qualitative observations. They help fill in parts of the personality portrait and may serve to stimulate further observation and research.

The competitive effort / Anyone can have a bad day. Hence, not all athletes who at times compete poorly can be considered poor competitors in the sense in which we are using the term. On occasion many athletes who have no chronic inability to compete will do badly in competition. This is especially true of them during the early parts of their careers. Yet even when the good and poor competitors make performances that are quantitatively similar, there are instructive differences in behavior.

An anxiety to do well can interfere with proper timing and execution of technique. Gross errors of anticipation are likely to be brought about by a full and violent effort to reach the goal. Good performance requires the proper execution of a series of integrated steps. Anxiety to achieve tends to disrupt this series, and there is a consequent poor performance. The normal competitor who has a bad day is usually the temporary victim of his overanxiety.

The competitive behavior of the poor competitor is remarkably different. There appears to be no interference with performance by an impetuous pull toward the goal. Instead, there is a feebleness of effort, almost a kind of paralysis.

As examples of contrasting behavior, the average high-jumper may do poorly in competition by rushing into the perpendicular plane of the crossbar, while the poor competitor simply makes a weak jumping effort. There seems to be very little error of anticipation by the poor competitor. The average pole vaulter who is having a bad competitive day will usually destroy the efficiency of his vault by increasing the violence of his effort; the poor competitor reduces the power or drive with which he leaves the takeoff spot. The distinction between good and poor competitors is seen even more clearly in the throwing events. When the relatively unblocked athlete makes a poor competitive throw, it is usually due to an anxious, inefficient effort with many errors of anticipation. But bad as it might be, the throw is made in a full and sometimes vicious manner. In contrast, the poor competitor's throw tends to be feeble and gentle.

This qualitative aspect of competitive behavior has diagnostic and predictive value. Let's assume that both A, the poor competitor, and B, the average or good competitor, have performed poorly in a given competition to about the same quantitative degree. A has performed in a semiparalyzed, feeble way. B has made many gross errors but has made violent tries. The outlooks for these two cases will be different. Subject A will probably remain a chronically poor competitor, but B may become an adequate competitor. His path to achievement is likely to be a bit thorny because he will be plagued by errors of anticipation. Yet, his outlook is generally good in that he is apparently not seeking to avoid athletic achievement.

Another aspect of the competitive pattern of the poor competitor is significant. He will often negate an otherwise adequate performance by an apparently unnecessary action. The thrower will foul a good effort by falling or stepping out of the circle when, from the standpoint of body mechanics, he can easily remain in the circle for a fair throw. The vaulter or high-jumper who has apparently cleared the bar with enough height will often, unnecessarily it seems, brush off the bar with his hand. Such a pattern is in sharp contrast to that of the good competitor who, in the face of a foul, will fight for body balance or squirm to keep every inch of his body clear of the crossbar. The long-jumper is in a good position to sabotage an accidentally good performance, since he can do it at either end. He can foul or fall back in the pit.

Attitude toward opponents / The good competitors seem for the most part to enjoy reasonably warm friendships with many of their opponents—but not during the actual competition. The situation is fairly well illustrated by the familiar behavior of professional boxers. During the actual boxing they attack each other viciously. At the final bell they embrace like long-lost brothers. But during competition, the opponent becomes a temporary enemy.

Both the ethics of competition and the traditions of sportsmanship preclude overt shows of hostility in most amateur sports. However, the good competitor reports hostile thoughts. In the field events, where trials are taken in turns, each athlete has a chance to concentrate on the efforts of his opponents. The use of the "evil eye" is a common practice. For example, a high jumper may report concentration on his opponent's foot slipping or the wind blowing off the crossbar. The discus thrower may concentrate on a possible foul for his opponent.

The recent death of a great competitive baseball player recalls his savage hatred of opposing pitchers. When asked about this hatred, he explained that "they are trying to take the bread out of my mouth." Apparently, he functioned best when he visualized the pitchers as enemies who were trying to starve him to death.

The good competitor may look forward to a number of "grudge matches." In such instances there may not even be a token show of friendliness. The athlete frankly states his dislike for his opponent and openly announces his intention of trouncing him. He appears to have little concern with possible counteraggression. One great competitor took particular delight in defeating an opponent because "this fellow gets so upset." Among a wide circle of opponents some personality clashes would seem inevitable, yet some of the good competitors may need a few "grudge matches."

The poor competitor prefers or may absolutely need an atmosphere of friendliness. The coach is sometimes startled and enraged to see one of his men offering not only encouragement but actual coaching aid to an opponent. When the good competitor offers "help," it is probably a form of gamesmanship, but the poor competitor's efforts seem to represent a genuine attempt to create a friendly atmosphere. By becoming friendly with an opposing good competitor, the poor competitor probably gains a relative advantage. The poor competitor does not have grudge matches. Even a practice duel carried out in mock anger can impair his performance. Teammates and coaches who try to motivate him by savage criticisms of the opposition probably lessen his achievement.

Practice pattern / Even though the finding is not significantly supported by the questionnaire responses, in the
cases I personally knew about, the poor competitors tended
to arrive at practice either very early or very late. An
individual sport, such as track or swimming, usually does
afford considerable flexibility in time, and to adjust for a
late laboratory or class, a squad member will sometimes
practice at an odd hour. But the poor competitor tends to
select a fringe hour without any compelling external reason.

The pattern of practicing at odd hours may meet a
number of needs of the poor competitor. If he manages to
arrive before the coach or after the coach has left, he avoids
a supervised workout. In general, the poor competitor
does not relate well to other people and likes to work
alone. Some poor competitors have been known to seek
other training facilities in the same area, such as high
schools, the YMCA, etc.

Since there are seldom close witnesses to the private
practices of the poor competitor, it's difficult to establish
what he actually does. But the few glimpses available
indicate that performances in private practice are often
vastly superior to anything that is done in the presence of
teammates or coaches. Evidence for such performances has
to come from sources like the reports of groundskeepers,
marks left by implements, positions of jumping standards,
etc. One athlete who barely made his college team had
private performances of Olympic level.

Method / Even when he has great experience in his event,
the poor competitor seems far more comfortable if he
works in the manner of a beginner. He prefers to keep
working on the material usually assigned to a first-year man.
He may report that he plans to move along to more

advanced material, but he must first "polish a few fundamentals."

Related to this practice pattern is one in which the athlete works hard, but in such a way as to prevent achievement. It is a startling thing to watch an athlete assiduously reinforcing a habit that is definitely known to interfere with good performance.

Both of these patterns may help the athlete to resolve a conflict. He can satisfy his need to work hard for achievement and still relieve his anxieties about actual achieving.

Search for Excalibur / In lieu of paying attention to principles and techniques that have a demonstrated relationship to successful performance, the poor competitor makes vague references to some secret and almost magical aspect of form. He seems to suggest that high-level performance will follow his acquisition of such a gimmick. This bizarre quest often dominates a large portion of the practice sessions. Naturally, the coach takes a dim view of such a procedure and is likely to step in. A gentle approach by the coach may evoke some sort of incoherent account of the athlete's search. Stronger methods are upsetting to the athlete and could result in his completely avoiding the coach or leaving the sport.

Off-season performance / In the out-of-season practice session, with competition not imminent, the good competitor usually has great difficulty approaching anything like his best performances. For example, the discus thrower who has reached 170 feet the previous spring may in his workouts the following October find himself struggling for 150 feet. But for the poor competitor the situation is reversed. He is usually at his very best in the off season, but his performance diminishes as the competitive season nears. There are instances of poor competitors actually approaching world records during the off season, only to become mediocre performers with the arrival of competition. The enthusiastic coach who extrapolates from the off-season performance of the poor competitor is due for a disappointment.

An eye to the future / It's no doubt true that nearly all athletes who do eventually reach high-level performance have along the way harbored fantasies about such achievement. They do not simply stumble into championships. Yet even when they have such long-range goals, they are able to concentrate, as they progress, on the subgoals, the imminent competition. Each successive competitive trial seems to be viewed as an opportunity to confirm the feasibility of attaining the big goal.

From time to time the poor competitors make vague references to their rather grandiose goals. They too have fantasies of great achievement, but it is a far distant achievement. They don't want to pay attention to the subgoals along the way. The next scheduled competition receives relatively little concentration. Their orientation is toward a very distant goal. Even when they are completing their careers, their athletic goals remain in the distant future.

Verbal behavior / The poor competitor routinely berates himself after each practice effort, especially if the coach is present. Almost before completion of the trial, the poor competitor will hang his head in a guilty fashion and reprimand himself. One gets the impression that he is trying to forestall criticism from the coach. In a sense he is trying to "beat him to the punch." Early in my coaching I made a persistent effort to eliminate this pattern. I tended in a naive way simply to view such behavior as an inefficient use of the athlete's time and energy. From a common sense point of view it seemed that they might best concentrate on something constructive. I never found these direct efforts to be even slightly successful.

In addition to his verbal pattern of self-condemnation, the poor competitor has a curious method of presenting an "argument" in his own behalf. He may begin with a defense of some technique or procedure that he's embraced and the coach has opposed. The arguments are at first presented boldly, then tentatively and with hesitation. Finally, even if the coach has listened sympathetically he withdraws the argument. All by himself he reaches the conclusion that his point of view is "really rather silly after all."

Negative approach / The *modus operandi* of most successful athletes is to concentrate on one or perhaps two positive points at a given time. They seem willing to accept the notion that one can work on a particular aspect of technique without being greatly concerned about making errors in areas that are not under consideration. Not so with the poor competitor, who appears constantly fearful of committing an error. His exaggerated concern with the possibility of various errors cropping up paralyzes his ability to take action on one or two positive points. Any reassurance given to the poor competitor that such errors are to be expected in the normal course of learning does not alter the pattern. In general, there is a strong suggestion that for the poor competitor the negative approach is not simply a matter of inefficient learning. Instead, it is a symptom of emotional inability to accept achievement.

Reaction to failure / By definition, the poor competitor competes poorly most of the time. Hence the typical reaction following competition is a reaction to failure, at least failure in the sense of the meaning of the word for most of us. The coach is often surprised to note that following a failure in competition the poor competitor is usually relaxed, in good spirits, and even talkative. In contrast, the good competitor who has had a bad day is difficult to live with. He becomes temporarily a bitter, morose, and sometimes unpleasant person.

Reaction to success / The poor competitors we have been considering are athletes of high physical potential, and thus on occasion their performances are good. The remarkable results of the questionnaire show that for the poor competitor success is inevitably followed by failure. Of sixty poor competitors not one was reported to have followed a good competitive performance with another good performance. Further, after a good showing they tend to fall off badly, performing even below their own competitive norms. In contrast, the good competitors are apt to follow one good performance with another. For them, success does indeed seem to breed success.

The reports of the coaches do show strikingly the poor competitor's reaction to success. Case studies go further by revealing the great emotional upset and distress that success can bring to the poor competitor. The following two instances illustrate some of the extreme behavior that can follow success.

A poor competitor of extraordinary natural physical talent was entered in two field events. His first effort in his first event went extremely well. Almost before he could prevent it, he had achieved by far the best effort of his athletic career. He appeared pained and anxious. His remaining trials were incredibly poor, but, of course, the first mark remained as his performance. When the time arrived for his second event, he was not to be found. Later it was discovered that he had left the athletic area in a panic. He could offer no explanation for his absence.

A pole vaulter routinely cleared twelve feet six inches in competition. Just as routinely, he failed to clear the next height, thirteen feet. Before the advent of the fiberglass pole, thirteen-foot vaulting could come in handy, as it often scored in dual meets. His teammates noted that he usually had more than six inches of clearance at twelve feet six inches and therefore reasoned that his inability to make thirteen feet was "only mental." Thus they conspired to help him. When his back was toward the takeoff, they raised the bar from twelve feet six inches to thirteen feet. Unaware of the bar's true height, the vaulter made a successful effort. In those days a vaulter's first clearance of thirteen feet was something of a milestone and tradition-ally called for a minor celebration. Thus, as the athlete landed in the pit and the bar remained aloft, his teammates rushed toward him with cries of congratulations. When he realized what he had accomplished, he was stunned. He immediately left the area and never again vaulted.

Both of these instances illustrate rather severe reac-tions to success on the parts of poor competitors. Reac-tions are not usually this extreme. More typically, there is a general loss in competitive effectiveness that may persist for several weeks or longer. Gradually, something like the normal level of competitive ability is resumed. In any event, though the severity of the reactions may vary, unex-pected achievement is a disturbing factor for the poor competitor. It seems that whatever anxieties prevent rou-tine good competitive efforts are doubly aroused by chance achievement.

Some other expressive behavior / Indications are that
the poor competitor is considerably constricted in the
expression of his aggression. Such constriction extends to
various facets of expression. Individual cases present
striking examples of "bottled up" personalities.

The poor competitor speaks very little. He practically
never initiates a conversation. I had the experience of
coaching one athlete for a period of four years without
once having a conversation with him. Nor, as far as I know,
did he ever converse with his teammates. He responded to
coaching instruction with nods or one word spoken in a
scarcely audible voice. On train or bus trips he would sit
alone and occupy himself with his books.   '

The poor competitor does not yell messages or call out
to teammates. He tends to speak in modulated tones. One
athlete spoke in such a soft voice that he could hardly be
heard at a distance of more than several feet. Any background noise would completely obliterate his voice.

The conversations that do take place between the
coach and the poor competitor are seldom satisfactory in
the sense that no "meeting of the minds" is attained. The
athlete does not seem to present any view in a coherent,
forceful, or logical manner. On the part of the coach there
is always the feeling that the athlete has not really expressed or revealed much of his own feelings and personality. Even after four years of acquaintance and observation, the coach may have only the haziest impressions
concerning the athlete's background. The poor competitor
makes little or no comment about his family. His mother
and siblings won't be mentioned. There is, however, a
suggestion at times of a strong father who "stands for no
nonsense" from the subject.

The ability to laugh separates the good competitor
from the poor. The latter is apparently unable to laugh in a

spontaneous or uproarious manner. He is only able to smile. It seems most extraordinary that an apparently simple bit of expressive behavior such as the ability to laugh out loud can have great diagnostic value. But it looks as if it's so.

What we seem to find about the good and poor competitors violates a cherished stereotype. We think of the cowboy who says very little but is quick on the trigger in a showdown. From everything we can make out, if he never got his gun out of the holster, he'd probably shoot himself in the leg.

Motivation / If, as it surely appears, athletic achievement brings about discomfort and anxiety for the poor competitor, the logical question arises: Why does he do it? Of course, for some generations there has been increasingly less surprise at the persistence of behavior that does not seem rewarding. The needs that bring a poor competitor to the athletic setting are not really known. However, a few comments on surface aspects of the motivation may be useful.

Most certainly there is nothing to justify a generalization that young persons with a fear of achievement in athletics will nevertheless be drawn toward participation in that area. On the contrary, it is reasonable to expect that athletes who exhibit such a pattern will eschew the area entirely. Then whom are we dealing with when we discuss the poor competitor? Possibly we are talking about one person in ten or less who, despite a neurotic fear of achievement, is drawn to sports. These persons may have a curious combination of mental and physical factors.

Testimony by athletes about their motivation is probably not directly valuable. Such testimony cannot always be taken at face value. Yet what is said can be illuminating.

Included in a questionnaire administered to an entire track squad was the question, "Why did you go out for track?" Among the group were several fine competitors along with two very poor ones. The answers of the good competitors tended to be terse and ran from such matter-of-fact formulations as "always liked it" to frank achievement remarks such as "thought my best abilities lay there, and I could do well." One of the poor competitors simply responded, "to help the team win the big ones." The other said, "spiritual stimulation of physical achievement and of being a member of a dynamic group . . . I also feel physical conditioning to be almost the duty of every man; this is why I chose a sport rather than a nonathletic activity."

Unlike the good competitor, the poor competitor avoids the expression of what might be viewed as "selfish" personal achievement needs. He cannot easily confront his own aggression. Instead, "higher" or more noble motives are cited. In this connection there is a striking similarity to Ernest Jones's account of the case of Paul Morphy. At the peak of his career, Morphy, perhaps the greatest chess player of all time, gave up the game. Eventually, he developed a psychosis. Jones believed that an important factor contributing to Morphy's downfall was the impugning of his "noble" motives by a major opponent.

Attempts to modify the pattern / The poor competitor creates the impression that he is afraid to "stick his neck out" (the analysts might use a different anatomical term), and his defenses are constructed to keep him from doing this. The defenses seem deep-rooted and strong. As far as I know, there is no certain documentation of a poor competitor ever becoming a good one. Attempts to modify the poor competitor's behavior only show the tenacity with which the defenses are held.

From time to time a situation can be created that makes the prospect of failure more uncomfortable for the poor competitor than the usual discomfort over the possibility of success. In search of a badly needed point or two, the poor competitor's teammates may almost force him to perform well. He may be told in the strongest terms that he *must* do well. He is given the threat that things will be made most uncomfortable for him should he fail. Under such circumstances a good performance can almost be "wrung out." However, if he does make a successful effort, his subsequent falling off is more severe than usual and may be accompanied by physical symptoms. The forced performance is likely to be the season's last good one.

The coach's pep talk is now pretty much out of fashion. When things go badly, the modern coach tends to concentrate on the technical errors underlying poor performance. Still, the coach does find a sustained disparity between physical capacity and competitive performance to be a source of great frustration. One coach told me about being plagued by a high-jumper who could always do six feet five inches in practice but had yet to clear six feet in competition. Prior to a critical dual meet the exasperated coach indulged himself in a strong pep talk, telling the jumper that he had been letting the team down. He concluded by offering the athlete the alternatives of clearing six feet in the next meet or turning in his uniform. The jumper did make six feet in the meet, and the coach believed that he had found a permanent solution not only for that particular case but for all similar cases. But the athlete never jumped six feet in competition afterward.

Further, he began to miss the five feet ten inches that was once habitual with him.

As previously suggested, the poor competitor's workout pattern differs from that of the normal competitor in several respects. Among these are his tendency to show up for practice at odd times and his further tendency to style his practice sessions so as to preclude achievement. I recall the case of one poor competitor who was so gifted in physical potential that he had to invent ingenious ways of avoiding achievement. Finally, I decided to abandon my usual permissive procedure and literally directed every phase of his practice sessions. Though I sensed that he was growing uncomfortable, his progress was truly remarkable. The only difficulty was that his name appeared on the next academic probation list, and he was ineligible for further competition.

Several years after I made this experiment, or, I should say, had this experience, my coaching colleagues in another sport reported on a poor competitor who seemed stamped with athletic greatness. For some two years this student had appeared for practice at odd hours, and each time he presented a plausible excuse. His unusual hours required some sort of makeshift workout schedule. His coaches reached the opinion that his failure to achieve was due to his peculiar hours. They investigated his classroom obligations and found that he could indeed attend practice sessions at the regular times. His excuses were without foundation. Armed with this information, they confronted the athlete and demanded that he report for practice on time and undergo the regular routine. They had him cornered. In view of my own earlier experience I was curious about the outcome of the case. The result wasn't long in coming. The athlete, a junior with no previous record of scholastic difficulty, made the next General

Warning list and was no longer allowed to compete. It could just as well have been an injury or an illness. Something would have done it.

Psychotherapy / The inability to compete well in athletics is not in itself sufficient reason for therapeutic referral. Yet the poor competitor may sometimes be referred for other reasons. I was familiar with the cases of three poor competitors who were referred for treatment. None completed more than a single psychiatric hour.

Psychiatry is an unusual type of medical treatment in that the patient has to have a flair for it. That's a bit unlike the patient with a broken leg who usually doesn't have to have a flair for having a bone set. But the flair concept does seem realistic in psychiatry. The poor competitor's lack of flair for psychiatry is probably involved in his unwillingness to have his defenses tampered with. No matter what the approach, no matter how glaring the evidence confronting him, the poor competitor will not outwardly entertain any notion that his inability to achieve involves an emotional problem.

In fact, he won't even concede that he has any difficulty in competing. He prefers little or no conversation with the coach. Especially, he is made uneasy by references to his competitive showing. If the subject is forced on him, he speaks of a future performance. At that time, he will have acquired the gimmick needed for success.

When pressed by his coach to achieve, the poor competitor may talk in a bizarre, even schizoid way. He may, for example, refer to his "poisoned blood" or to his hamstrings that were shortened by some mysterious disease. Yet it seems that the poor competitor seldom is diagnosed as a psychotic. On the other hand, I do know of two athletes who competed well for a time and who also become schizophrenics. Both were given leaves of absence from college, one of them being hospitalized. The interesting aspect of these two cases is that both were achievers with personality patterns suggestive of the poor competitor. For example, though both exhibited considerable verbal behavior, their speech seemed to represent something of a strain. They appeared to be playing some sort of artificial roles. One of the two never laughed at all, while the other laughed in a mirthless, artificial way. Upon returning to school, neither resumed athletic activity. One hastily informed me that his crowded schedule prevented him from participating further. He appeared much relieved when I quickly accepted his decision.

Speculations and questions / The pattern we've been talking about is essentially one in which the subjects are drawn toward athletic participation and yet are blocked in their achievement. A fairly consistent personality portrait begins to emerge. In general, the poor competitor is badly constricted in other modes of expression.

For some reason or reasons athletic success is anxiety-provoking, and such success is warded off by a system of defenses that is held with great tenacity. The two above-mentioned cases of psychosis suggest that in a sense the poor competitor may be "correct" in maintaining his defenses in the face of the immense pressures upon him to do well in athletic competition. Should he relinquish his defensive system, he might be overwhelmed by his anxieties.

Freud, when he wrote about people who are "wrecked by success," and Jones, when he explored the downfall of Paul Morphy, may have been dealing with the same pattern we've been looking at. Both relate the fear of achievement to the oedipal situation. It's understandable that their explanations should be within the analytic framework. There may, it seems, be other and different determinants, such as the nature of the inherited nervous system, and biographical factors other than oedipal ones.

One significant question is concerned with the implications of the poor competitor's personality in dealing with other areas of life. Does the poor competitor suffer from a disability that can cause him misery after school or college? It would be surprising if such a powerful system of defenses has meaning only in the context of athletic participation.

A somewhat optimistic clue may be supplied by the ability of our subjects to achieve normally in the academic area. Some of the poor competitors have been good students. Since there are individuals who can achieve academically but not athletically, some comparison of the two areas is indicated. One major difference suggests itself. Athletics have been traditionally masculine activities, whereas the academic area represents a rather neutral pursuit. Perhaps the constricted behavior of the poor competitor derives partly from his general fear of "sticking his neck out" in a masculine endeavor. He may be relatively free to express himself in a more neutral or possibly even in a traditionally feminine activity. We might hypothesize that the degree of vocational disability suffered by the poor competitor will depend upon the nature of his occupation. The more masculine the occupation, the greater the disability.

The needs of the coach and the needs of the poor competitor are obviously in direct conflict. In most sports settings the coach feels that his mission is to win contests, and the athlete who could be great except for "that queer mental quirk" is a painful source of frustration. Great hostility can be directed toward the athlete. Physical disability is readily understood and tolerated, but an emotional disability tends to be perceived as cowardice. The coach who becomes hostile toward the athlete is as little suited for his job as the psychiatrist who shows hatred of his patients. However, the responsibility of the coach to the poor competitor is a complex matter, involving value judgments and requiring more knowledge than we have now.

An Added Word

It's hard to think of two areas that are more intriguing than sports and psychology. An interaction between them would seem bound to produce fascinating results and views. Yet the remarkable growth of sports psychology appears to be taking place without much contact with formal psychology. In some ways the sports psychology movement has quasi-spiritual aspects. One thought seems to be that we have long neglected the athlete as a person, and that we must make up for this long-standing sin. However, at the other extreme, there is the view that we may squeeze a better performance from the athlete through the use of psychology.

A vigorous interaction between sports psychology and formal psychology will, I feel, be slow in coming about. There are difficulties on both sides. Many people who have backgrounds in either coaching or physical education have seized upon the popular word "psychology" without having much notion of what the term means to professional psychologists. Some coaches and physical educators think of psychology as anything from an inspirational talk on motivation or clean living to shrewd observations on how to keep the locker room orderly. These very topics have been the subjects of "sports psychology" publications. Yet there are those who realize that there must be more orientation toward formal psychology.

Though the structures of both coaching and psychology present obstacles to a useful dialogue, the greater difficulties may lie on the side of psychology. The area of psychology is a formidable one to approach and grasp because of its mountains of literature, its various schools, and its many divisions. It would seem more realistic to refer to "psychologies" rather than to "psychology."

The movement toward a sports psychology has originated in sports rather than in psychology. The initiative in establishing a more active relationship between sports and psychology will probably have to be taken mostly by the sports people. But such an effort is needed if there is to be a viable and valid field of sports psychology.

Index

Academic institutions
  and athletics, 2–3, 36, 82–88
  and prediction of performance, 123–27
Academicians, inferiority feelings of, 37–38
Adler, Alfred, 34–35, 38–39
  See also "Individual psychology," Adler's
Age
  life-style and, 39–42
  and sports activity, 4–5, 8
Aggression, 70, 185
  poor competitor and, 200, 201, 204–5, 212
Alumni, coach and, 87–88
Amateur vs. professional sports, 6–9, 137–39
American Psychological Association, 21
Animals
  Darwinism and psychology's view of, 45–47
  laboratory observation of, 44, 47–56, 58–62
  wild, training of, 55
  See also specific animals
Anticipation, errors of, 165–75
  coach's handling of, 171–74
  poor vs. normal competitor and, 202–3

Apes, Köhler's studies of, 61–62
Apperception background, 188–91
Aptitude, 114–22
  scholastic, 115–17, 123–25
  sports, 117–23
Archimedes, 163
Aristotle, 13
Atomic bomb, 181–82
Auto racing, 154

"Balance" and aptitude, 119–20
Bannister, Roger, 178
Baseball, 143–44, 153, 205
  anticipatory errors in, 166–67
  "problem boxes" in, 125–27
  professionalism in, 6–7
  strength training in, 148–50
Basketball, 144, 150, 184
  aptitude scores and, 123
  professional, 6–7
Behavior modification, 89–90
Behavior of Organisms, The (Skinner), 53
Behaviorism, 15, 20–21, 49, 52
  maze experiments of, 59–60
  Pavlovian theory and, 49–56
  Skinner's, 53–56
Binet, Alfred, 116
Boxing, 154, 184, 204
  professionalism in, 7
Brumel, Valery, 182

Carnegie, Dale, 95

Carr, Bill, 179–81

Catholic Church, 32, 33, 42

Cats, experiments with, 47–48, 59

Character structure, *see* Personality

Chicks, Thorndike's experiments with, 48

Chimps, Köhler's studies of, 61–62

Christian Science, 43

Christianity, 20

    See also Catholic Church; Protestantism

Clarke, Ron, 182, 183

Clubs, athletic, 83–84

Coach, 82–112

    and alumni, 87–88

    and anticipatory errors, 171–74

    apperception background and, 188–91

    and athletes' life-style problems, 38–42

    and athlete's resistance, 97–103, 110–11

    and college administration, 85–86

    compared with teacher, 56–59

    football, 88, 93, 96, 114, 145–46

    inferiority feelings of, 36–37

    and mental rehearsal, 160–62

    and operant conditioning, 56–59

    Pavlovian theory and, 52–53, 55–56

    personality of, 90–92

    and poor competitor, 193–94, 201–2, 205, 207–9, 212, 215–17, 219–20

    prestige of sport of, 134–36

    and "problem athlete," 102–12

    psychological confusion in, 93–95

    and psychological limits, 176–77, 183–84

    and regression under stress, 144–46

    relationship with athlete of, 94–112, 162

    and retroactive inhibition, 150–51

    rise of, 82–85

    and role playing, 154–58

    and selection of personnel, 113–14

    surveyed on competitive ability of athletes, 194–202

    technical competence of, 88–89

    track and field, 88–89, 91–92, 99–102

Colleges, *see* Academic institutions; Ivy League

Communications breakdown, coach-athlete, 98–100

Communism, 20

Compensation for physical inferiority, 37–38

Competitive ability, 192–220

    attitude toward opponents and, 204–5

    competitive effort and, 202–4

    expressive behavior and, 212–13

    goal orientation and, 208

    motivation and, 213–14

    off-season performance and, 207–8

    practice pattern and, 206–7, 216

    psychotherapy and, 217–18

    questionnaire survey of coaches on, 194–202

    reactions to failure and success and, 209–12

    verbal behavior and, 208–9, 212

Conditioning

    operant, 54–59

    Pavlovian (instrumental), 50–56

Copernicus, 20

Counselors, 103

Crew, 135–36

Cross-country running, 135, 136

Crows, 46–47

Cults, 43

Darwin, Charles, 20, 45–46

Demosthenes, 35

"Depth" psychologies, 42

    See also Individual psychology, Adler's; Psychoanalysis

Descartes, René, 14

Desire, *see* Motivation

Dickens, Charles, 67

Discus throw, 119–20, 169, 172, 184

Dogs, Pavlov's experiments with, 49–56

Dreams, Freudian theory of, 27
Dropout, motivation of, 138–41
Dumas, Charles, 178

Effect, law of, 48, 58–59
Ego, 29–30
Einstein, Albert, 20
Endurance and aptitude, 121–22
England, *see* Great Britain
Environment, human nature vs., 3–4
Evolution, theory of, 45–46
Experimental psychology, 16–17, 187
    and personality, 67
    See also Behaviorism
Extinction, Pavlovian concept of, 50, 51

Faraday, Michael, 20
"Fictive goals," 35, 38–39
Fonville, Chuck, 179
Football, 150, 153, 184, 185, 193
    age and, 4
    anticipatory errors in, 165–66
    coach in, 88, 93, 96, 114, 145–46
    prediction of performance in, 127–28
    professionalism in, 6–8
    regression under stress in, 144–46
    U.S. popularity of, 133–34
    use of sled in, 150–51
Free association, 25
Freud, Sigmund, 20, 24–27, 32–34, 45, 67, 183
    Jones's biography of, 32
    See also Psychoanalysis
Fuchs, Jim, 179

Galileo, 20
Gestalt psychology, 15, 61–62
Golf, 6, 8, 144, 165
Great Britain, 178
    coaches in, 83, 85
Greeks, ancient, 137
    character structure and, 66
    as early psychologists, 13
    sports striving and, 2
Gymnastics, 154

Hammer throw, 36, 148
Hartshorne, Hugh, 68
Helmholtz, Herman von, 163
High jump, 58, 148, 171, 192–93, 203, 204, 215–16
    anticipatory errors in, 168, 170, 172, 173
    records in, 178, 181, 182
Hockey, 133, 154, 184
    age and, 5
    professionalism in, 6–7
Human nature, notion of, 3–4, 13
Hurdles, 6
Huxley, Thomas, 45–46
Hypnosis, 25, 185

I.Q. tests, 116
Id, 29–30
"Individual psychology," Adler's, 34–35, 38–39, 42
Inferiority feelings, 35–38
Inhibition, 181, 183–85
    retroactive, 147–51
Instrumental (Pavlovian) conditioning, 50–56
Intelligence, measurement of, 116–18
Introversion-extroversion, 67, 68
Ivy League, 139
    coach and athletic policies of, 86
    prestige of crew and, 136

James, William, 14
Javelin throw, 143, 169
Jesus Christ, 32
Jews, 33
Jones, Ernest, 32, 214, 218
Jung, Carl Gustav, 34, 67, 68

Köhler, Wolfgang, 61–62

Landy, John, 178
Learning theories, 45, 147
    See also Behaviorism
Life-style
    Adler's concept of, 35, 38–39
    of athletes, 38–42
Lifetime sports, 5, 8

Limits, psychological 176–85, 193
    See also Competitive ability
Long jump, 167–68

Masculine striving, 9–10
May, Mark, 68
Maze experiments, 59–60, 169
McGill University studies, 25–26
Mental rehearsal, 159–64
Morphy, Paul, 214, 218
Motivation, 129–41
    competitive ability and, 213–14
    cultural factors in, 132–34
    definition of, 130–31
    of dropout, 138–41
    mental rehearsal and, 161
    need for prestige and, 136–41
    physiological maturation and, 131–32
    and poor competitor, 200
    prestige of sport chosen and, 134–36
Murray, Henry, 79

Nazis, 32–33
Neuroses, 174
    operant conditioning and, 56–57

O'Brien, Parry, 178–80, 193
Olympic Games, 10, 36, 177
    coaches and, 89, 91–92
    records set at, 179–82, 193
On the Origin of the Species (Darwin), 45
Operant conditioning, 54–59
Owens, Jesse, 181

Paper and pencil personality tests, 76–77
Pavlov, I. P., 49–50
Pavlovian theory, 49–56
Pelé, 115, 134
Perception, 186–88
"Personal Data Sheet," Woodworth's, 67, 76
Personality, 63–70
    coach's, 90–92
    competitive ability and, 194–200
    definitions of, 64–65

literature and, 66–68
    traits, 65, 67–70
    types, 69–70, 90
    See also Personality tests
Personality tests, 63, 67, 70–81, 103
    paper and pencil, 76–77
    projective, 71, 77–80
    rating scales, 74–76
    reliability in, 70–73
    validity of, 73–74
Philosophy
    influence on everyday life of, 20
    psychology and, 13–14, 187
Pigeons, 54, 60
Plato, 13
Pole vault, 57, 106–7, 203, 204, 211
    anticipatory errors in, 169–71, 173–75
Poor competitors, *see* Competitive ability
Prediction of performance, 114, 116–17, 122–23
    in academic context, 123–27
    past performance and, 123–28
    See also Aptitude
Prestige
    athlete's need for, 136–41
    of sport chosen, 134
Principles of Psychology (James), 14
"Problem athletes," 103–12
"Problem boxes," 124–28
Professional vs. amateur sports, 6–9, 137–39
Projective tests, 77–80
    Rorschach, 71, 78–79
    TAT, 79–80
Protestantism, 33–34, 42
Psychiatry, 23, 217–18
    See also Psychoanalysis; Psychotherapy
Psychoanalysis, 15, 20, 23–34
    and academic psychology, 27–31, 42
    personality theories of, 67
    as religion, 24, 31–34, 42
Psychological limits, 176–85, 193
    See also Competitive ability
Psychology, 12–34

amateur, 13, 23
animals and, 44–62
"depth," 42
early history of, 14–15
Gestalt, 15, 61–62
"individual," Adler's, 34–35, 38–39, 42
learning theories of, 45, 147
modern development of, 15–17, 20–21
philosophy and, 13–14, 187
product and influence of, 19–20
psychoanalysis and, 15, 23, 27–31
specialization in, 15–16, 18–19, 21–22
training in, 17–19, 28–29, 59–60
See also Behaviorism; Experimental psychology; Psychoanalysis; *and specific concepts*
Psychometrics, 79
Psychosis, 214, 217–18
Psychotherapy
analytic, 25, 26
and poor competitor, 217–18
See also Psychoanalysis
"Puzzle boxes," 47–48, 58–59

Quantification in psychology, 49, 60
Questionnaires
on competitive ability, 194–202
on motives for pursuing sports, 214
in personality testing, 76–77

Rat experiments, 54–55, 59–60, 169
Rating scales, 74–76
Reality testing, life-style and, 39
Record explosion, 178–84
Regression under stress, 142–46
Reinforcement, 54, 57
Reliability in psychological tests, 70–73
Resistance, athlete's, 97–103, 110–11
Retroactive inhibition, 147–51
Richards, Bob, 170
Role playing, 152–58
Rorschach, H., 78
Rorschach test, 71, 78–80

Roosevelt, Theodore, 35
Russia, 2, 9
Ryun, Jim, 182–83

Scientific method, psychoanalysis and, 27–31, 42
Scholastic aptitude testing, 115–17, 123–25
Sex in Freudian system, 26–27
Sexton, Leo, 179
Shakespeare, William, 16, 67
Shot put, 10, 99–102, 120, 169, 193
records in, 178–80
retroactive inhibition and, 148–50
Simpson, O. J., 115
Skiing, 154
Skinner, B. F., 53–54, 56
See also Operant conditioning
Skinner box, 56
Sled, 150–51
Soccer
age and, 4
cultural factor in popularity of, 133–34
professionalism in, 7
Social workers, 34
Sociologists, 31
Sociometry, 43
"Speed" and aptitude, 120
Stimulus and response, 20–21, 60
See also Behaviorism
Strength
and aptitude, 120–21
effect of stress on, 142–45
Strength vs. technique training, 148–51
Stress, regression under, 142–46
Success, fear of, 131, 175, 201, 210–11, 218–19
See also Competitive ability; Psychological limits
Superego, 29–30
Swimming, 92, 154
age and, 5, 155

Technique vs. strength training, 148–51
Tennis, 8, 154
anticipatory errors in, 166

Tests
  intelligence/aptitude, 115–17, 123–25
  reliability of, 70–73
  validity of, 73–74
  See also Personality tests; Projective tests
Thematic Apperception Test (TAT), 79–80
Theophrastus, 66
Thomas, John, 182
Thorndike, Edward Lee, 47–48, 61
Torrance, Jack, 179
Track and field, 154
  age and, 4, 5
  anticipatory errors in, 167–75
  coach in, 88–89, 91–92, 99–100
  psychologists' preoccupation with, 89, 105
  record explosion in, 178–84
  survey of competitive ability in, 194–202
  women in, 10
  See also specific events
Traits, personality, 65, 67–70
Transfer of training, 151, 190

Unconscious processes, 24, 174

dreams and, 27
and mental rehearsal, 16'–63
United States
  athletic subsidy system of, 2–3
  rise of coach in, 82–85
  sports culture of, 133–34
Universities, *see* Academic institutions; Ivy League

Validity in psychological tests, 73–74

Warmerdam, "Dutch," 170–71
Watson, John B., 52
Wealth, national, and sports activity, 2–3
Weight lifting, 143, 154
Wild animals, training, 55
Williams, Ted, 167
Women, 10
Woodworth, R. S., 67, 76
Workout
  poor competitor and, 206–7, 216
  resistance to, 99–101
Wrestling, 144, 154
  age and, 4

Yale University, 52–53
Yachting, 5